DEVELOP YOUR PSYCHIC POWERS

BOOKS BY EILEEN CONNOLLY

TAROT: A NEW HANDBOOK FOR THE APPRENTICE
(THE CONNOLLY TAROT, VOL. I)

TAROT: THE HANDBOOK FOR THE JOURNEYMAN
(THE CONNOLLY TAROT, VOL. II)

THE CONNOLLY BOOK OF NUMBERS, VOL. I: THE
FUNDAMENTALS

THE CONNOLLY BOOK OF NUMBERS, VOL. II: THE
CONSULTANT'S MANUAL

EARTHDANCE (A novel of reincarnation—an introduction to
metaphysics)

KARMA WITHOUT STRESS: CONNOLLY ESOTERIC
GUIDEBOOKS, VOL. I

DEVELOP YOUR PSYCHIC POWERS: CONNOLLY ESOTERIC
GUIDEBOOKS, VOL. II

Forthcoming:

TAROT: THE HANDBOOK FOR THE MASTER
(THE CONNOLLY TAROT, VOL. III)

KARMA, NUMBERS AND THE DESTINY OF CHILDREN

CONNOLLY ESOTERIC GUIDEBOOKS:
    VOL. III: FORMS OF HEALING
    VOL. IV: THE BODIES OF MAN
    VOL. V: THE MYSTICAL GATE
    VOL. VI: APPROACHING THE CABALA

CONNOLLY ESOTERIC GUIDEBOOKS
VOLUME II

DEVELOP YOUR PSYCHIC POWERS
THE BASIC TOOLS OF PARAPSYCHOLOGY

EILEEN CONNOLLY

NEWCASTLE PUBLISHING CO., INC.
North Hollywood, California
1990

Edited by J. Kelley Younger
Copyedited by Ann McCarthy
Cover/Book Design by Riley K. Smith

FIRST EDITION
A NEWCASTLE BOOK

10 9 8 7 6 5 4 3 2
Printed in the United States of America

DEDICATION

To my little brother Tommy, who deftly wove the thread of karma into an outstanding life pattern. Second chances were never given; maybe that was the reason for his beautiful outlook on life. He came as a Christmas gift and left on a bright summer day that held his smile long after he left.

My big brother Tom was a mountain of strength. He loved life and expected no one to contribute to his destiny. I will always remember him standing at my door, and his silent power was a light that went too soon. Tom was life, and life was short. His difficult karma was complete and those left behind still wonder why.

ACKNOWLEDGEMENTS

To my readers throughout the world, the scholars, teachers and others. We are sharing another adventure of study. We will be exploring the many paths to inner wisdom. We will be spending time together and during this time I want to share your excitement and progress.

To old and new readers, I extend my gratitude for the ongoing strength I receive from you all. I would like you to feel I am teaching you personally, so that the book becomes not only a source of learning but a friend you can relate to on a very personal level.

Whatever your purpose in studying the esoteric arts may be, this work will provide you with a continual ready reference. It contains both theory and procedure to explore the vast field of parapsychology.

—Eileen Connolly

CONTENTS

CHAPTER 8

CHAPTER 9

CHAPTER 10

CHAPTER 11

CHAPTER 12

CHAPTER 19

LIST OF ESOTERIC EXERCISES

THE CONNOLLY
ESOTERIC GUIDEBOOKS

This series of guidebooks is designed to provide good comprehension plus a format of basic study. As with all my books, my intention is to teach you as simply as possible how to work with and understand the basic esoteric concepts. Whatever your purpose in studying may be, the guidebooks will provide you with a continual ready reference. Both student and teacher will find the series interesting and informative, as each volume provides its own unique learning tool.

This series opens the mind to the basic concepts of Parapsychology. It allows the reader to explore the rudiments of esoteric principles, and provides a format of approach and learning for the serious scholar to discover the esoteric Missing Link.

PREFACE

You can turn your life around completely by expanding your personal ability. Learn how to use all the energy coiled up inside. Many of your hidden talents are tightly tangled with resistance and emotional blockages. Learn how to separate and evaluate this living power. Allow your conscious mind to see beyond your present horizons. Take personal command and break all your preconceived limitations! Explore your world beyond the barriers of logic and discover new spheres of possibility.

Unfortunately, there is a tendency to exclude the possibility of being psychic simply because one appears to have not been "born" with psychic powers. But the foundation required to support your search is merely a firm belief that with good basic principles of knowledge, plus the personal determination to study and apply these principles, the field of Parapsychology is open for the seeking scholar.

Psychic ability is similar to any other ability. It is not a broad field of expression for everyone. Within the field of Parapsychology you may discover that you have a talent for one particular aspect of psychic expression. In much the same way, a college student does not have the capacity to major in *every* subject a university curriculum has to offer.

Being psychic does not mean that you are an expert in the field of Parapsychology. You may have a natural aptitude for one particular facet; however, this does not represent the vast area of esoteric expertise. Generally speaking, people are given credit as a psychic when, in fact, they practice according to their own capabilities—thus presenting a mere fraction of possibility in the field of Parapsychology as a whole.

The preconceived concept of being "psychic" or "not psychic" should be eliminated, to allow the seeking student to discover his own particular gifts. Trying to develop your psychic ability in every possible area will defeat the whole idea of development. The secret is to find your own natural abilities and focus directly on your own psychic expression.

"To each his own" should be the motivating principle. Discover where your psychic talents lie. A good clue would be your personal reaction to any subject matter. If, for example, you feel extremely intuitive, it could be that you have the natural basic talents of a clairvoyant. Follow your intrinsic curiosity. Maybe you feel compelled to study a specific subject. Follow this inclination and you may discover that you have an inherent psychic ability.

Developing your psychic ability is like any other educational project. One must approach the subject through the application of study, interest and concentration. Once you have acquired a basic level of knowledge, then it must be applied and tested with patience and discipline.

In this day and age there are many competent teachers who can help the student become proficient in his chosen subject. Many aspects of Parapsychology are linked in such a way that one field of interest leads to another. Finding that very first link is the beginning of any serious venture into esoteric areas.

Everyone has their own specific link. This book is to help you find your Missing Link.

—Eileen Connolly
Virginia
April 1989

INTRODUCTION

Psychic Development begins immediately when you start your personal search—the moment you realize there is a possible extension of your capability over and beyond your everyday Consciousness.

Where to begin is always the question of the serious student. There are many schools and many teachers, but you feel the need to do some personal research—to get an idea of what is possible and to understand fully what type of studies are available. Most important, of course, is where do your psychic talents lie?

Before this wonderful exploration can take place, you must prepare yourself. There are many ways, some of which might hinder your early progress. Exposing yourself to discussion groups too early can be off-putting, as the participants may be already immersed in the various psychic activities.

Let me suggest an initial and satisfactory approach to making your psychic début and finding your Missing Link:

1. Prepare within yourself. Clear the way by contemplation and meditation (see *Karma Without Stress*, Vol. 1 of this series).

2. After you have completed the preliminary clearance, have an open mind and begin your search. This can be done by reading or making inquiries through an established school or teacher in the field of esoteric philosophy.

3. The above preparation can be done alone or by forming a group of people who are also searching for information about Psychic Development.

4. A good esoteric teacher reading this work might consider offering the above procedure for serious seekers who are beginning to explore the possibility of Psychic Development.

CHAPTER ONE

THE PSYCHIC

The word *psychic* comes from the Greek word *psychikos*—of the soul, spiritual. *Psyche*, the soul. *Psyche* is a Greek word for mind, Consciousness, and was originally used to denote the force of life within man. When used in modern times it refers to mental faculties of the Conscious and Unconscious Mind. The word *psychic* is commonly used in reference to people who are apparently sensitive to forces or energy beyond the physical world.

In a sense, then, we are all psychic, for we all have a soul. It is within the power of man to avail himself of his own soul qualities. There are people who are seemingly born with the ability to use these inherent gifts and we normally consider these unique people to be natural-born psychics. This is not to imply that any particular measure of intelligence can be attached to this inherent ability. The application of intelligence comes from the working Conscious mind and is not part of being psychic. There are natural-born psychics who are highly intelligent, but they would still be intelligent if they were not considered to be psychic. Too often a parallel is assumed, though it should not be.

A psychic scholar is a beautiful combination of two separate levels of Consciousness blended successfully. Unfortunately many psychics live on an isolated level socially, and because of the mystery surrounding their profession they are not challenged or treated in the same way

1

as other advisors. Generally speaking, people are reluctant to ask pertinent questions as one would with any other professional counselor. A lawyer or doctor, for example, is constantly questioned to enable the client to fully understand where the knowledge or information comes from. In the case of a psychic, this does not always happen.

A psychic receives information not generally known. The source of this knowledge is vitally important. This brings up another aspect, which is the esoteric source of information. Many practicing psychics have a guide, master, angel, deceased relative, etc., who provides guidance and gives information that would otherwise be unobtainable through normal means. Some make no claims regarding the source of information received. Still others acknowledge the Universal vibratory force and say that by using psychic ability, they are able to extract information from it. Is all this possible? I feel very strongly that it is! I am a natural-born psychic and I know these things to be true.

I also know that the source of information a psychic uses should be analyzed and verified! If we are to believe in outside forces, and these forces have lived on earth at some other time, then one must consider the validity of such forces. A simple example might be, if Uncle Joe passed away, and during his life he was an habitual liar, why then should any credence be placed on his messages?

A psychic should always be aware of his source and should not hesitate to use all his means to check information received. There are higher forces that can be relied upon. Directing energies through higher levels of Consciousness would inevitably establish a good and positive reliable source.

This, then, is the psychic who receives and transmits information for the good of others. We usually refer to the psychic who receives this type of esoteric communication as being a *medium.* A medium can receive information in many different ways, such as a *clairvoyant—* one who sees; a *clairaudient—* one who hears.

Another aspect of mediumship is through the use and technique of Divination, which is the act of foretelling the future by means of interpreting various representations of symbolism. Tarot, Fochaadams, *I Ching* and Runes are a few of the divination tools that can be used to delve into the higher realms of Consciousness. Through the given symbols one is capable of penetrating the Higher Consciousness. The actual skill of the person would determine the caliber of information received. Here is an example of ability plus intelligence.

A psychic, then, is a medium who is able to extract hitherto-unknown information and predict future happenings. The method or tools of the psychic determines the way in which the psychic receives the given information. Any serious attempt to pierce the unknown has to be considered a psychic endeavor. A person who reads Tarot cards and develops his ability as a Tarotologist is also using his psychic ability plus his normal intelligence.

Regardless of how someone gains contact and obtains information that is not considered normal, they are using a psychic ability. We will be exploring several accepted psychic outlets. If you feel a strong attraction to any of the areas then you should study, practice, and apply intelligence to qualify all information received.

APPLYING PSYCHIC ENERGY

Every single day we apply psychic energy to our daily activities. We do this in so many ways that it is impossible to define when and how. The mother who knows when something is wrong! Making a phone call at just the right moment! Suddenly deciding to change travel arrangements! These are just a few simple examples of psychic ability being used.

People we do not normally associate with esoteric knowledge or competence may very well be using their psychic talents. I personally know of a great lady with no esoteric training who is very definitely a competent esoteric astrologer. Whenever we use another sense to expand and go beyond the accepted theories we are using our psychic abilities. Even "common sense" often stretches beyond normal behavior patterns. How often have you been forced to use such "common sense," and then felt glad that you did?

Psychic energy should not be considered a force available only to special people. It surrounds us all and is available to all. To some, it is comparatively easy to access. For others, it requires study and training. Whichever category you are in, one thing is vitally important and that is the *skill* to use your psychic talents.

To become more sensitive you must eliminate all existing negativity. Various procedures can be used to achieve this necessary level. I recommend you use the meditations and exercises in the first volume of the Connolly Esoteric Guidebooks, *Karma Without Stress*. It is seldom realized that the negative tendencies existing in our everyday Consciousness prevent us from reaching the correct level required for Psychic Development.

Once the mind is clear and you are willing to accept your present position, the karmic path will present many avenues of esoteric expression. As you study the procedures remember that it takes time to develop to the level you desire. In many cases, it has taken a lifetime.

Have patience with yourself and know that each step you take brings you nearer to your original goal. Even if you are presently using your psychic abilities, you may find the organized basic approach advantageous. Teachers also can use this structured curriculum for their new esoteric students. If you are now exploring for the very first time I welcome you to the wonderful possibilities of personal Psychic Development.

BEGINNING YOUR PSYCHIC DEVELOPMENT

Psychic Development begins with a whole new outlook on life—a new and fresh approach. This is accomplished by first erasing all negative tendencies and replacing your Conscious level with bright new possibilities; extending your thought process beyond your own immediate needs; and not limiting your thoughts to yourself, to your home, or entirely to your work situation. You are quite an expert at doing this already!

For this exercise, instead of allowing your thoughts to flit here and there, try to focus your attention entirely on another person. This person should not be emotionally close to you. It should be a person that you know little or nothing about. Maybe someone who lives down the street. Someone you saw in a shopping center. Perhaps a person in the office that you have not had much contact with.

This exercise will take you out of your normal thinking process. Once you are able to do it with little or no problem you are well on your way to Psychic Development. All you need is a Conscious image of the person you are going to focus upon. From this point you are going to stretch your mind and place your normal thinking process onto the image of a person you do not know.

Watch out for your own mind interference! Simply because the Conscious mind does not have any information to tussle and toil with, it will try very hard to place your concentration elsewhere. If and when it does, just gently refocus and ignore the automatic pull from your Conscious level.

EXERCISE 1: LONG-RANGE FOCUS

1. Just relax in a chair or lie on the couch and bring the image of the person directly to your Inner Eye (this is at the top of the nose between the eyebrows).

2. Without any undue effort, see this person as you have seen them before.

3. Now change the expression of the person. See them smile, and hold that picture for a moment.

4. Now see them laugh and, if you can, imagine you can hear them laughing. Again, hold this for a few moments.

5. Still looking at the face, now see the person looking relaxed and preoccupied. Try to feel the energy surrounding the person.

6. Feel, if you can, the pull of their responsibilities. How does it feel? Are they happy? Yes or no?

7. Do you like what you feel?

8. Is this person content? What are they looking forward to?

9. Now flood your image with WHITE Light and imagine your Inner Eye gently closing.

10. Did you actually feel the vibratory energies of this person?

11. Were you able to retain your Long-range Focus?

Experimenting with this exercise can help you initially to project your Conscious mind beyond its normal range. Just going outside yourself and placing your focus directly on another energy is valuable.

When we sleep, the Conscious mind is rejuvenated. When we daydream we experience the same therapeutic effect. The Long-range Focus exercise will alert your Higher Consciousness to participate. On finishing this exercise, write down your experience and don't allow the Conscious mind to interfere. Write in your journal immediately and refuse to record anything from your normal Conscious level. Soon you will become quite good at Long-range Focus. The value of this exercise is twofold:

1. It takes the focus off yourself and you can experience the shifting of energies as you put one hundred percent focus on someone you do not know very well.

2. Secondly, continuous practice of this exercise will soon accelerate your Psychic Development. Once you completely master the technique of deliberately extracting your own thought process and transfering your energies to another, you will actually begin to tune into the vibratory force surrounding the person. Thus you will be attuned to a vibratory force outside your own. This unique feeling is a sure sign of activity on a Higher Level of Consciousness.

CHAPTER TWO

THE SECRET OF BASIC ORDER

The natural law of "Order" plays an important part in Psychic Development. This fact is often ignored, yet without personal order and discipline it is virtually impossible to be attuned to the Higher Energies. The desire to develop the esoteric senses is not enough in itself. When you consider exactly why you want this to happen, it all becomes crystal-clear.

Man is surrounded by disarray in everyday activities. To begin his spiritual growth he must first have control on his present level. This requires personal discipline and effort. To achieve any success in Psychic Development one must work from a Point of Balance. Obviously it is not possible to correct every situation. Life is full of constant challenge. Let us consider what is possible and what is necessary.

EXERCISE 2: THE TEN POINTS OF INITIAL BALANCE

1. Recognize everything exactly as it is at this time.
2. Accept situations you cannot change.
3. Begin immediately to change what you can change.
4. Make new solid foundations and realistic goals.

5. Nurture these goals daily and refuse any negative influences.

6. Have complete faith in yourself. Believe in yourself.

7. Take a new interest in your physical health.

8. Accept who you are and understand your own needs.

9. Remember why you are doing these things. Remember your desire to develop spiritually, and take full command.

10. Balance is the key, balance in everything. From this point you will develop your psychic ability and find your "Missing Link."

Your Ten Points of Initial Balance provide a bouncing board to success. These ten vital points of discipline will strengthen your life daily. Keep a copy handy and check each day to make sure that you are following the path to your future success.

Understand the law of Order. To achieve access to the Higher Level of Consciousness, one must be in firm command of life. Only from this Point of Balance can you elevate yourself to the Higher Energies, and know without doubt that your solid foundations will provide what you need to develop true psychic ability.

THE POWER OF CONCENTRATION

There are many areas of life that are not available to all of us. A particular skill or talent may be required, thus we become disqualified to participate in a certain area. But strange though it may seem, there is one vital power that everyone can use. This power can change your whole life! It is the Power of Concentration.

Great spiritual teachers like Jesus, Moses, Confucius and Buddha used the Power of Concentration to achieve miracles. To concentrate is to collect or focus one's thoughts, efforts, etc.; to increase the strength, density or intensity; close or fixed attention. To do these things in everyday living is to have the ability to concentrate at will on any aspect of life.

The mere act of concentration brings about a magnificent force which the Conscious mind extracts from the Universal Energies. Normally, the Conscious mind deals with many activities. Consequently it is continually interrupted. The Power of Concentration is initiated when the Conscious level is forced to exclude other thought patterns. Just by refusing to let go of your focus, you automatically have access to the Higher Consciousness.

As you prevent your Consciousness from pursuing its normal function it immediately changes direction. The Power of Concentration stimulates the Higher Consciousness, causing the Universal Energies to initiate and produce the desired results. Prolonged and regular acts of concentration will establish a new and vital power within you—this wonderful Power of Concentration!

THE ART OF VISUALIZATION

The Power of Concentration by itself is not usually considered an effective means of obtaining what we need in life. It is a powerful force that can bring results. But simply knowing how to avail yourself of this power is not sufficient.

A vital ingredient is needed. This ingredient is the ability to visualize. Without Visualization the Power of Concentration becomes inadequate. Visualization is the psychic step taken after imagination. Children use their imagination freely and, because of their intensified concentration, they can actually experience an esoteric reality. Children develop the sequence of their imagination as they play. Each situation is manufactured at the time of Visualization. After they withdraw from the experience, they leave it suspended for further access. We refer to this as "make-believe" or "childish imagination." So it is, and the child escapes into the reality they have created almost at will. Unfortunately, and unknowingly, children soon close the doors to the wonderful world of childish possibility. We are pliable and flexible, and without too much resistance, we soon learn other means of play.

The art of Visualization provides access to the Power of Concentration. For some adults it is a comparatively easy procedure. Others may find it difficult to let go of familiar patterns of restriction. These restrictions are sometimes self-made and sometimes imposed by obligations and relationships.

To become a real expert at Visualization is quite simple. Using pen and paper makes it considerably easy. Imagine you are writing a screenplay. List your CHARACTERS and describe the background, scenery and the SITUATION. Briefly describe what you want to happen—the STORY. The less detail you have, the clearer the Visualization will be. You may have to add things here and there and also erase unnecessary details. Once you are very clear about what you want, your Visualization can be put to use. Let's begin with a step-by-step procedure.

EXERCISE 3: USING YOUR OWN POWER

1. Get a clear and concise picture of what you want. Write the details down. We will call this picture your PLAN.

2. When you decide exactly how you want things to happen, think of your plan frequently. Anytime, anywhere, let your thoughts touch upon your plan—washing dishes, relaxing after dinner, etc. Don't waste any valuable spare time! The more energy you contribute to your plan the easier your Visualization is going to be.

3. *Energy Spots* are the times when you can be alone and quiet. Choose at least two Energy Spots a day.

4. Feeling relaxed, focus directly on your Plan, resisting the urge to let your thoughts stray.

5. Now visualize the situation you have created. FEEL YOUR FOCUS AND YOUR VISUALIZATION MERGE. As this takes place you are in the process of using your psychic energy. As the FOCUS and VISUALIZATION MERGE you are in the act of using your Power of Concentration, which will begin *instantly* to work toward your PLAN.

6. Hold this level as long as possible, for you are now using your Power of Concentration. Every *second*, you are in the act of manifesting your PLAN.

7. In a short time your Higher Consciousness will take over and start to extract the energy needed for your plan from the Universal Force.

8. Remember to visualize a real and living picture. See it all taking place. Feel yourself in the center of your PLAN. Know

without any doubt you are creating your own Power of Concentration and you are making your PLAN manifest.

Thinking things out prior to making your final Plan will determine how quickly your Power of Concentration will work for you. Try not to make your Plan too busy. Make sure that it is entirely focused on one particular issue. Putting too much detail in the picture necessitates extra energy and a longer period of time before you realize the results. As you advance and become adept at using your Power you can have two different Plans working for you at the same time. You would of course have to allocate extra Energy Spots. You will need a minimum of two Energy Spots a day for each Plan.

One might consider the time involved as being more than beneficial. Constant practice of reaching to your Higher Consciousness will not only result in maturing your Plan but will also become an essential part of your whole Psychic Development. Taking charge of your life and being a part of your own decision-making puts you in command. From the command position you can then make choices and build firm and solid roots for your future.

CHAPTER THREE

SHARPENING THE INTUITION

Natural feelings and awareness really do play a big part in your Psychic Development. Intuition is something we are born with. It is a sense of direct knowing without the conscious use of reasoning. Generally speaking, people avoid using intuition. They have not learned to rely on their natural instinct. Unless the Conscious level has proof, it tends to reject the intuitive reaction. Intuitive knowledge is often discussed after the act. Smilingly, someone mentions how they knew something before it happened. It's almost thought of as an unusual streak of thought. That's because it doesn't seem to happen very often.

As an essential part of your Psychic Development, you must make note of these kinds of occurrences. Let me explain why your intuitive feelings are important. At all times, your Higher Consciousness is transmitting data to your Conscious level. On rare occasions the everyday Conscious level gives way to the input of the Higher Energies. This seems to happen especially when something traumatic is taking place, though at other times you might receive insignificant information for no apparent reason.

What is going on? We have two simple examples, Traumatic and Non-traumatic. How do such intuitive powers function without your apparent control?

First, you must accept that your intuition is a part of your Psychic Development. Whether or not you consider yourself intuitive is not important. Everyone has intuition. How does it work and how can you encourage it to work?

RECEIVING

The Universe is buzzing with information. Your television set is in the corner of the room and, unless you turn it on, it has a blank screen and is totally silent. If you turn it on, you will have both vision and sound. A modern miracle, you might say. A proficient engineer could explain how it works, but to the uninitiated it remains a miracle. Apparent miracles are soon taken for granted. People watch television and listen to radios without a second thought. Yet these same people have difficulty accepting psychic phenomena.

It's important to remember that the possibility of each new thing discovered, from electricity to the complexity of present-day technology, has always existed. Before it was known, the possibility existed. Esoteric energies exist also, and as man progresses, new ways of using these powers are acknowledged every day. When man discovers new and wonderful techniques, he is using brainpower plus intuition.

The Conscious level is usually busy thinking of this and that. During normal work or business, you apply whatever is necessary to complete the job. If you are fortunate enough to be doing exactly what you want and earn your living through the use of your natural talents, then you are combining brainpower with intuition.

Everyone has inherent talent. But most people never achieve their potential. Many would-be artists, authors, musicians, for example, are lost to the world, because of social background and karmic destiny. Nevertheless, the potential still exists. This knowledge is available in the Higher Consciousness.

You may feel that you have an unused talent, but that your present lifestyle prevents you from exploring it. Surrounded by your obligations, you manipulate quite an amount of energy in denying yourself the opportunity to investigate your inborn talents. This is the Conscious level at work.

Glimmers of intuition occur when the Higher Self feels you should be aware of a particular situation. Traumatic circumstances seem to paralyze the normal thinking process momentarily. When this happens, the Higher Consciousness presents and emits a different energy form. This form or thought structure is actually a kind of "knowing." In what would seem to be a fleeting second, the normal level of Consciousness receives hitherto-unknown information.

Through this Higher Energy form you can also receive contact from souls who have passed over from this life. This usually happens when you are tired or asleep. Often the impact is strong enough to awaken you. Swiftly, the Higher Energies allow both vision and sound, because you are sleeping and you don't resist the incoming force.

When the body is totally relaxed in sleep the Higher Self is better able to function. As the body feels the surge, it is suddenly awake and is able to comprehend the reason for the impact. If you remain asleep, then the force of the energy influences the dream process, which leaves an unquestionably vivid memory when you wake up.

EXPANDING YOUR WORLD

It is surprising how many people live within their own self-limitations. Like a horse wearing blinders, a person goes forward not seeing left or right. Exercising the Conscious level can take us beyond such restrictions. Expanding your world this way is an exciting step in your Psychic Development.

You are never too busy to take this next step. The next time you look at a flower, expand your world. Think of the color, the perfume, the shape and nature's nourishment that created the flower. Go beyond what you normally perceive. See a child as a soul with a karmic destiny. Think of all the potential and future purpose of the child. Try to feel the hidden talents and past wisdom the soul has experienced. Stretch out and expand into your new world.

Ask yourself questions and try to open your mind to your Higher Consciousness. Try to discover who you are, what you brought with you from another life. Be fully open to the feelings of others. See if you can sense a bond between you. Have you been together before? Take a long look at where you live. Does it feel right? Have you possibly lived here before? If not, where else have you lived? If you had the complete freedom to live wherever you wanted, where would it be? Now don't listen to your Conscious level. Go beyond that, break any barriers, and allow your Higher Self to take you exactly where you belong. Refuse to take things for granted. Probe and enjoy rediscovering your own expanded world.

When you look in the mirror you see a reflection of yourself. Look carefully into the face. Is it happy? Or do you look depressed or uninteresting? The way you look is how others see you. If you are not very impressed, then start now and change how you think and how you feel. Your reflection will show you how well you are expanding your world.

COMFORTABLE CELL

Just how comfortable is your cell? Are you surrounded with a dull feeling of content? Do you rock in your chair of acceptance and disconnect yourself from your true feelings? Are you afraid to open your Door of Opportunity? Can you hear the success of others outside? Is this your life? Is this what you want?

Controlling your life is a necessary step to Psychic Development. From the center of who you are, a power extends that denotes a mysterious vibratory identity. You are known by your "light." This light is the measure of life effort. Like a flame, this light reaches out to spiritual dimensions. The Higher Self is energized by this flame and the Conscious level merges with the Universal Force.

Is your comfortable cell small or restricting? To continue your development you must step outside the Door of Opportunity. Your karmic destiny is waiting. If you feel locked in because life has not offered you very much, understand that life is not your benefactor. Opportunity is all around. It comes, it touches, and then it moves on. You must be there to grab it. Examine every possible opportunity, and examine it well. There is no penalty if you feel it is not for you. Another, and another, will always be near. Too many people became disenchanted because they missed an opportunity. Life is absolutely full of opportunities but you will never know that if you remain in your comfortable cell.

Think of all the people who have known success. The secret of their success was in recognizing opportunity. One thing leads to another. You must make that very first effort. Don't be afraid it will be stolen from you; everyone is not looking for the same opportunity! As you expand your world, you expand your enthusiasm and your inner strength. It is never too late to begin again—and again, and again.

Come out of your comfortable cell. Breathe the fresh air of new opportunity. Nothing is going to change unless you make it change. You can turn your whole life around by first recognizing what a wonderful soul you are. Think of the many cruelties you have inflicted upon yourself. Put more joy in your life. Material things are not made of joy. The substance of the soul animates every deep desire. It's time to live, it's time to start again. Now, right now, begin to clear the way for your new Psychic Development. After all, if you can't control your life on a day-to-day basis, how can you expect to open your Higher Consciousness for great and wonderful situations?

Open your Doors of Opportunity. Discover new situations, new faces, the new "you." Be alert to everything that crosses your karmic path. Look, think, analyze and then decide. Use your new strength and it will bring the power you desire. It doesn't matter how much or how little you have; this is the first rule. What really matters is that you are renewed, refreshed and full of new energy. Age doesn't matter, money doesn't matter. But *you do*.

Come out of your comfortable cell. Look straight ahead and see the beauty all around you. Consider everything that you once took for granted. Evaluate what you have, and know that everything is possible if you are willing to recognize your own spiritual power and identity. The world is big. Have you been content with your small comfortable cell? Clear your vision, open your ears, and taste your new spirituality. Let go of your fears. Be prepared to do something about your life. Change things today, and tomorrow will bring you closer to your goals.

Do everything you can to clear your karmic path:

Apologize.	Forgive.	Let go.	Give back.
Change jobs.	Be free.	Forget.	Start again.
Move away.	Go back.	Begin again.	Don't be afraid.

Smile.   Relax.   Have faith.   Expand your world.

Change.   Take action.   No regrets.   Love yourself.

Add to this list any other aspect of your life that needs attention and healing. The minute you act on these things, you will escape from your comfortable cell. Simple meditation procedures will completely erase any remaining negativity. (See *Karma Without Stress*.) There is so much in life to enjoy and explore.

Now we are on an open plain of true possibility. We have much to see and understand. You are ready to begin your Psychic Development. Remember, opportunity is not something that happens only to other people.

CHAPTER FOUR

ORACLES

An Oracle is a divine announcement received from a deity, by and through a medium or priest. At the Temple of Apollo, at Delphi, Apollo's priestess was called the *Pythia*. This name referred to the enormous python that Apollo killed when he first came to Delphi. The Pythia would enter a state of trance and the temple priests would interpret the information (oracles). Visitors to the temple would ask questions about the oracles and the priests would give the answers as the Pythia received them. It is said that, in her trance, the Pythia received her wisdom directly from Apollo.

Obviously, this priestess was a medium. She went into trance and the voice of Apollo gave information to those seeking his wisdom. Oracular technique is used in various Divination procedures. After learning how to use your Divination tools, your intuitive senses begin to develop. By asking pertinent questions and then using a Divination procedure, the selected tools of Divination provide a way for you to translate the answers using your intuitive powers.

THE MEDIUM

A medium allows the mind and body to be taken over by an entity. This method of contact requires specialized training and also a great deal of faith in the spiritual source. A medium learns to develop a relationship and an understanding with a spiritual being.

The nature of the mediumship also varies. Some mediums have a group of entities who relate their own type of information. Others may have just one spiritual companion or guide. The entity usually has a specific purpose in manifesting himself through a medium. It might be healing, philosophy, guidance, or being the mediator between the two worlds. In a case like this, the medium is able to open up and allow different spirits to come through, and relay messages of support and/or importance to the person seeking information.

A medium with these spiritual abilities is normally referred to as a *trance medium*. There are many other kinds of mediums. Each has its own specialty of communication. The trance medium seldom uses Divination tools. This medium is able to transfer his Consciousness in such a way that the spirit can use the medium's physical body for speech, healing, etc.

During the time when the incoming spirit occupies the medium's physical body, the soul of the medium is often taken elsewhere. Usually they have no knowledge of what took place physically. In my years of research, many mediums have told me about special places they are taken to, like a garden, or a resting place. Some refer to the schooling they receive, and others have mentioned beautiful places of healing and rejuvenation.

As you can see, this type of mediumship is really for the purpose of helping others. The medium gains a sense of satisfaction from this kind of activity. It could be considered a vocation, because the medium devotes his talent and abilities to those seeking his help. Having no knowledge of the wisdom given can, of course, be rather frustrating. Nevertheless, there are many mediums who enjoy this type of spiritual vocation. If you feel inclined to know more, you should make a point of going to a reputable source for information and/or training. Having a natural gift is not satisfactory in itself. A good runner needs to train to become an athlete. In the same way, I recommend you direct any inquires about trance-medium development to an established professional source.

I feel quite strongly that a true trance medium has specific natural tendencies. Fortunately, in the field of parapsychology there are respected and dependable teachers and training programs to assist people. A student can become confused if he does not realize that he has an entirely different gift from the one he is studying.

Clairaudience, for example, is the esoteric ability to hear voices. Joan of Arc had this gift. Such voices cannot be heard by anyone else. Difficulties can arise when a student is actually showing a gift of clairaudience, then somehow there is a shift in the Conscious mind and the clairaudient feels compelled to add the spoken word. When this happens the would-be medium becomes confused and feels pressure. Knowing that he can hear someone trying to make contact, the student may struggle, attempting to induce his own trance-like level.

This is why it is important to seek professional advice and training. A good teacher can determine exactly which psychic potential the student may have, and offer a suitable training program.

There are two distinct fields of esoteric communication:

1. Natural Mediumship

These are mediums with natural abilities of mediumship. They have direct communication with spirits. They demonstrate this competence through the various types of mediumship.

2. The Oracular Method

Others use the Oracular method of Divination. They communicate with spirits using various selected tools of Divination to instigate and establish a liaison. They interpret information and wisdom from the spiritual source through these tools.

The essential difference between these two methods of esoteric communication is that the natural medium makes a direct contact. The other reaches the identical source but uses Divination procedures to translate and determine the information and wisdom received.

One important factor used in both these procedures is intuition. To use intuition you must be clear of self-imposed negativity. I cannot stress how much more you will develop your sensitivity if you use the preliminary exercises. Further exercises and meditations (see *Karma Without Stress*) can be used to eliminate remaining negative tendencies.

CHAPTER FIVE

THE PHILOSOPHER'S STONE

There are numerous, perhaps countless, ancient Divination procedures. Some of these methods are still used, while others have faded over time. As man developed, he adapted some of the old procedures by finding contemporary Divination tools to achieve similar purposes.

Perhaps the most mysterious of all divinatory practice is the art of Alchemy—the ability to transform base metals into silver and gold. We know that the ancient Egyptians were excellent metalworkers. They had great knowledge and believed that there were esoteric properties that caused a mystical change when particular metals were combined. This process required the use of the Philosopher's Stone, a mysterious technique that reached its peak during the Middle Ages. Essentially related to occult interpretation, Alchemy had three separate aspects: Heaven, Earth, and Man.

Although it is known that Alchemy was tested and used, it was veiled by utmost secrecy by the actual practitioners. Through the centuries some have claimed a measure of success in transmuting basic metals. Alchemy is considered by many experts to be the forerunner of chemistry as we know it today.

Evolving from this secret technique we can see the complexity and possible origin of esoteric practices. The Philosopher's Stone contains the essence of life and is a unique symbol. We know the Alchemist considered that the Philosopher's Stone held the actual elements from which all other metals originated.

Time, and the nature of man, make subtle moves that are often undetectable unless studied in detail—a shifting of beliefs and a gradual merging of one unknown aspect into another; an unwillingness to let go of an original unexplained concept and a gradual transformation providing a new insight. In the meantime, the clock ticks through the centuries and gradually another theory is born without appearing to have threatened or demolished the original. This took place with the Philosopher's Stone.

There are really *two* Philosopher's Stones, one used in the ancient art of Alchemy, and the other containing the mystical essence of life. Yet, they are one in the same! But time has mysteriously veiled the original practice of Alchemy. So reluctantly, esoteric scholars through the ages have looked upon the Philosopher's Stone as a vessel holding the sacred secret of life.

From these two theories the serious student can see how man throughout time has consistently endeavored to reach the God essence both practically and spiritually. The mystical union of spirit and matter has been recognized and placed in an esoteric symbol we know as the Philosopher's Stone.

Many interesting works have been written about the ancient Philosopher's Stone. Some people have claimed to be successful in changing basic metals. Others place a great emphasis on the spiritual aspect.

YOUR PERSONAL PHILOSOPHER'S STONE

Choosing a stone or a rock, and recognizing the essence of God within, can provide you with a strong spiritual tool. Touching the rock or meditating with it, visualizing the essence of life existing within, could be the foundation of your Psychic Development.

A rock comes from nature. It is not easily broken; it represents strength. Unlike a flower that soon fades away, the rock remains firm and solid. Hidden inside is the essence of creation, a part of who you are—for the essence of the divine is in everything. Using your own Philosopher's Stone is creating your own mystical symbolism. It becomes your personal spiritual representation.

The light of a candle shimmering on your Philosopher's Stone can be quite uplifting. It becomes an important focus point. The decision to have your own Philosopher's Stone depends, of course, on your ability to recognize the possibility. It is like looking at a photograph of someone we love. Our affectionate look and tender feelings are not aroused by the actual photograph—it is what or who the photograph represents. Your Philosopher's Stone would act in the same way.

It represents strength and purpose, protection and wisdom. It is used to enhance other spiritual activities. Your own Philosopher's Stone is a personal symbol that does not require the belief of others—just as people use lucky charms and other objects to focus their feelings. It is not a holy instrument or relic, but rather a starting point of spiritual communication. From the source and spiritual power of your stone you can widen all possibilities on your karmic path. You can build new towers of personal strength. Fresh and exciting goals can be established. Future motivation can be inspired.

All these can be had when you use something you can hold and see. Religions use spiritual tokens for personal faith and strength. Whatever your personal choice or religious persuasion, all such tokens offer that Missing Link. Your choice can be your Philosopher's Stone.

CREATING YOUR OWN PHILOSOPHER'S STONE

The first thing you need to do is find a stone that you feel is suitable to use as your personal Philosopher's Stone. Select it with care as you will be using this stone for a long time. Whatever you find appealing will work for you. Look for your stone in the mountains, on the beach or in the countryside. If you prefer to purchase something extra-special, there is a tremendous supply of crystals and rocks in stores everywhere.

Either way, select a substantial stone, and one that looks exactly as you would visualize your Philosopher's Stone to be. Take your time and be sure that you get exactly what you want. If you purchase your

Philosopher's Stone, you can explain what you are looking for, and they will undoubtedly be able to obtain it for you.

Your stone should have a significant place in your home. By that I mean it should not be tucked away. After all, displaying an attractive stone could be considered a part of your décor. Decide first where you will put your stone, then start your search. The decision as to where the stone will be placed is important. Your Conscious level submits this information to your Higher Consciousness and you will feel this inner guidance when selecting your stone.

The stone should be placed on a wooden stand, the kind used for expensive vases and ornaments. Cover the top of the stand with a small WHITE cloth,[1] on which you place your Philosopher's Stone. After obtaining your stone, prepare it according to the procedure in the following exercise.

PREPARING THE STONE

Wash your stone in tepid water. The old-fashioned way of preparing the baby's bath is excellent—test the water with your elbow. You should not feel heat or cold. The temperature should make the water almost undetectable as it touches the skin. Use a light dishwashing liquid and a soft washcloth.

Then rinse the stone in tepid water. A spray bottle is perfect. Or you can place the stone in a sieve and rinse with running water. After it is rinsed thoroughly, have a clean WHITE towel ready and place your stone on the towel. Bring up the corners and wait until it is dry. Once the stone is dry, you can gently wipe it all over with your "stone cloth." Use your stone cloth to remove dust daily. Your Philosopher's Stone should be attended to each day and kept clean. A surface of dust impedes the vibratory energies emanating from the stone. Constant dusting of the stone is like renewing esoteric batteries.

[1] You may use a cloth in your Soul Color, instead of a white cloth, if you wish. To determine your Soul Color, see *The Connolly Book of Numbers, vol. 1, page 33.*

The original cleansing procedure should be repeated annually, ideally prior to the annual Transition Period. (See *The Connolly Book of Numbers*, vol. 2.) During this period, the changing cycles can affect your stone. The annual cleansing process rejuvenates the Philosopher's Stone and ensures that its energy does not vary.

EXERCISE 4: STONE RITUAL

This beautiful esoteric exercise represents the coming-together and unification of man and spirit. The focus begins when the Conscious level accepts the personal Philosopher's Stone as a place or receptacle of spiritual light. The Higher Self is then better able to function, as it transfers and releases energy to your chosen source. For this exercise, you will need the following:[2]

1. Four WHITE candles.
2. One WHITE cloth.
3. One PURPLE cloth.
4. Small dish of cold water.
5. Small WHITE hand towel.
6. A PURPLE pillow.

The word *ritual* means a set form, a prescribed manner of ceremony, used to placate a deity—a formalized behavior involving a desire to obtain blessings and spiritual gifts.

Choose a time when you can be relaxed and enjoy creating your Philosopher's Stone. In group study the teacher could have the students obtain their stones and select a special date for conducting this ceremony. It is beautiful, enlightening and enjoyable. The collective energy from a group of esoteric students can create a magnificent vibratory experience.

---

[2] You may use your Soul Color instead of white for the purple cloth and pillow. To determine your Soul Color, refer to the note on page TKTKTK.

The spiritual atmosphere of love and joy in establishing your own Philosopher's Stone is rewarding whether you do it alone or with a group. Selecting a special day also has its advantage. It becomes the birthday of your Philosopher's Stone, and if you share another special occasion on the same date, it makes it all the more significant.

You may want to burn your favorite incense and/or play some special music. Before you start, make sure that you are not going to be disturbed. Disconnect the phone if necessary. Bathe before you begin, dress loosely and lightly. Read the following prayer *before* you conduct your ceremony:

PRAYER

I am cleansed in my body. I am ready to cleanse and purify my soul. I pray to God that any negativity remaining will be purified and never return. I am a child of God and I know in my soul I am loved and protected. Take from me any existing doubts, dear Father. Release all my fears so that I may know Your heavenly Light.

I know the Divine Spirit is everywhere, within me and around me. I seek to focus my attention on my path of destiny. Too often I have strayed from my path in fear. I seek the Light. Too long I have been in the shadow. I am now ready and I ask this day that my spiritual vision be clear. I pray for Your holy blessing in every aspect of my life. Fill, dear Father, my body, mind and spirit with Your everlasting love and wisdom.

Before me is a Stone. A symbol I have chosen to find the true gift of spirituality. Today I start my journey back to Thee. With this Stone I will be ever-mindful of Your holy Presence. When I look at this Stone and when I touch this Stone, may I always be aware of the Holy Spirit and my faithful promise to You this day. I am weak but in Your love I am strong. I know You are everywhere for all time. I come now for spiritual comfort and strength. Let this Stone be ever-blessed and surrounded only with my pure thoughts and actions. Within my Stone I extend my Holy

Temple. I ask that my pure intention be blessed, and my Stone be a living reminder of the Divine Love, Wisdom and Power. May all those who recognize my Stone receive Thy Love and Power forever. Amen.

FINAL PREPARATIONS

Important: During this ceremony you must be facing East, the direction of the rising sun. This has always been considered beneficial by esoteric scholars, as it means facing the direction of "the most pure representation of the first emanation from God."

1. Place your PURPLE cloth in the center.
2. Surround the cloth with four WHITE candles.
3. Know the positions of North, South, East and West.
4. To the left, place a bowl of water and a clean WHITE hand towel.
5. Place the PURPLE cushion for kneeling.
6. To the right, place your stone, wrapped in WHITE cloth.

If you burn incense, place it in the East position, beyond the candle.

SOLIDIFYING THE STONE

1. After the Prayer, light each candle and repeat the following:

   "With the power of God I reach to the furthest North of Existence."

   "With the power of God I reach to the furthest South of existence."

   "With the power of God I place myself to the holiest of all existence. I humbly request that I be purified in mind, body and soul so that I may remain in the source of the First Light."

"With the power of God I look upon all that I have been. I ask for forgiveness and ask that the holy Light from the East fall upon me and remain with me at all times. Amen."

2. Take the stone from your right hand, still wrapped in WHITE cloth. With your left hand, put your fingers in the bowl of water and shake the water over the covered stone. Do this three times.

3. Now blow out each candle in turn, starting with North, then South, East, and West.

4. Holding the covered stone, say:

"I focus directly to the center of this Stone. I seek the Essence of Light within."

5. Uncover the stone and drop the WHITE cloth behind you. Reverently place the stone on the PURPLE cloth in the center of the unlighted candles.

6. Dip your left hand and your right hand simultaneously in the bowl on your left, saying:

"As I cleanse my hands, my soul reaches out to pure Light."

7. Gently dry your fingers on the WHITE hand towel.

8. Re-light the candles, beginning with North, then South, East, and West.

9. Repeat: "With the power of God within me, and the everlasting Light around me, I now illuminate my existence."

10. "I am Thee I am, I am Thee I am, I am Thee I am. Amen."

11. "I will bring this Light to the Living Light within the Stone."

12. Stretch out your arms high over the Stone, with palms facing down, saying:

"I now bring this Light to the Living Light within the Stone."

13. Wait for a few moments. Allow the new Light to expand to every part of your body. Feel the energy come through your arms, into your hands, and radiate down into the stone.

14. Kneel on the PURPLE cushion. With palms open and facing up, visualize yourself in the center of the Stone. (Wait.)

15. Feel the Light pulsating around you. Feel the power of the Light penetrating each tiny crevice within the stone. (Wait.)

16. Let your sincere need for Light expand into the stone. Become the very center of the stone. Fill the stone with your love of life and desire for Light and true understanding. (Wait.)

17. You are the center of the Light. You are the source of spiritual power and knowledge. Feel yourself now with much power, slowly growing to your normal physical size. You are glowing with the radiance of glowing White Light.

18. See yourself burst forth into a rainbow of magnificent brilliant colors. The spiritual force thrusts you forward and you are now facing your physical body.

19. Now step boldly into your physical self. As you do, feel immediately the powerful surge of pure White Light enter every part of your body. (Wait.)

20. You are the living Light from the stone. You have now brought this Light to every part of your being. You are filled with new wisdom. YOU ARE THE PHILOSOPHER OF THE STONE. You now have the key to improve your life. (Wait.)

21. You are the key. You are the Philosopher. You are the Living Light within the stone. Your new spiritual strength will bring you the wisdom of your karmic path. All that you can accomplish is a part of the new Light that surrounds you. Within the stone is the pure reflection of your soul. The purity of your existence is the essence of God. It is protected deep within your Philosopher's Stone. (Wait.)

22. Repeat: "I am a part of the Universal Force. All that I am is pure Light, Love and Spiritual Power. I am the true Philosopher and my Stone contains the reflection of my self. Within my Stone is all wisdom and knowledge. My soul remains in the pure, untouched Light of God."

23. Standing facing the stone, blow out each candle in turn. Pick up your stone and, lifting it high, repeat:

"I am Thee I am. I am Thee I am. I am Thee I am. I am the

Light within my Stone. I am a part of every living thing. I joyfully allow the God energy to rise within me. I am full of spiritual strength and power. I will use my strength and power to guide me in all things. I no longer have fear. I am Thee I am. I am Thee I am. I am Thee I am. Amen."

24. Put the Stone down and say: "I am the Philosopher. I am full of wisdom. This is my Stone and I will protect the pure spiritual flame that now burns within. This is my true spiritual pledge. This is my Stone."

(Exercises and meditations are available on tape. For further information see Appendix.)

CHAPTER SIX

DIVINATION THROUGH THE AGES

Many of the ancient methods of Divination have survived into our modern world. Others have been lost through the centuries. This happened mainly because the particular divinatory tools used are no longer a part of our Western culture.

The old Divination practices are very interesting. One old Celtic method was *Hippomancy*. This form of Divination required the esoteric skill of analyzing or interpreting a horse's gait.

Another divinatory practice was known as *Gyromancy*. The person walked around and around in a circle. The circle had symbols at various points. The walking continued until the person became dizzy or collapsed. This was the exciting part of the Divination, for at this point, the corresponding symbol or letter indicated the desired prophecy.

Belomancy was possibly one of the oldest methods of Divination. It was the ability to foresee the future by using arrows. *Austromancy* was the skill of Divination by the movement, speed and direction of the wind.

If you study the older methods of Divination, you will discover many interesting procedures relevant to the age in which they were used.

Fortunately, many have survived through time and are still considered favored methods of Divination. People commonly consider Divination to be related to a natural or inherent skill. But many of the divinatory skills were handed down from generation to generation. The person had to *develop* his intuitive ability, as well as learn the actual practice. So it has always been. Psychic Development in any form has to be a combination of intuition and "know-how."

The ancient procedures of Divination that are no longer practiced are countless. Each era, each period of time reveals the various tools of Divination used. As man progressed his tools became more and more refined. The art of *Spodomancy* was the gift of seeing special omens from the strange shapes that soot or cinders formed. The heat would cast quivering color tones and the flames flicked in and out of the cinders and soot. The combination of heat and flame created pictorial cameos, depicting future events.

Geloscopy was a divinatory form used by listening to the pitch and sound of someone's laughter. *Tasseography* is the art of reading tea leaves. The many shapes form mysterious patterns and omens. After the drinking of the tea, the dregs are swirled around and the cup is then turned over onto the saucer. When this little ceremony is complete, the leaves left in the cup are then interpreted and read.

Reading tea leaves has long been an exciting form of Divination especially in England, where tea is still made in a teapot, the old-fashioned way, with the actual tea leaves. But you can see that if people are not accustomed to making tea this way, it would be hardly likely to use Tasseography for Divination.

So one divinatory form has given way to another throughout the centuries. Yet certain Divination procedures have not succumbed to time and we have to ask why. You will see that most of the dying arts of Divination were associated with the tools of the time. Many of these practices were considered natural psychic talents.

At the same time there were other esoteric procedures that required a measure of knowledge. Intuition alone was not sufficient. Usually the information was considered secret and information was handed down through families or learned from special esoteric schools.

The actual arts of certain divinatory procedures require a certain level of sensitivity. It is this sensitivity or intuitive quality that triggers the initial esoteric spark. Learning the nature of the tool, along with the art of esoteric interpretation, can provide much depth in a reading. We have now determined that the various Divination procedures did not necessarily have identical approaches. Some were considered inherent and others required a certain amount of schooling. This does not make any one form or practice better than another! The result and accuracy of a reading is what really matters.

So it is important to understand and appreciate any natural psychic ability you may have. And to realize that even though you may have an inherent psychic gift, certain divination procedures must be learned and adapted to your intuitive qualities.

SPECIALIZED ESOTERIC SKILLS

I am sure that many of the teachers reading this work will agree when I say that there are specific esoteric skills that require specialized study. A client requiring pertinent information can select a proficient counselor or teacher specializing in all the many areas.

If a person needed advice he would select a counselor. He would be able to select from a wide field of esoteric expertise. The information received would be very similar, regardless of what type of Divination was used. Each individual skill would depend on the counselor's knowledge plus esoteric skill.

Each counselor would use his or her own unique combination of intuition and knowledge. Consequently, some would appear to be better than others. It is important to remember that the actual souce of wisdom and knowledge is the same! Each practitioner, using their personal specialized skills with their chosen esoteric tools, extracts information from the Universal source. There are essential points that make the consultation differ: the nature of the inquiry; the type of Divination used; the esoteric skill and proficiency of the practitioner.

THE NATURE OF THE INQUIRY

Depending on the nature of the inquiry, you would usually direct a query to a particular type of esoteric counselor. You may be attracted to a divinatory procedure and want a consultant proficient in that technique.

For example, a client wanting to know more about astrological aspects would seek out an astrologer. Another person may want information about a relationship, and have a Tarot reading. Maybe you notice unusual lines in your hand and you want to know more. Then, of course, an appointment would be made with a person who knows Palmistry.

When we consider areas of Divination like these, we know that the person we select to give us the information has a good reputation and proven skills. This does not cancel out the "plus" they may have—the extra boost of psychic or intuitive ability used along with their academic skills.

On one occasion when I met a new student, and we talked about her natural intuitive abilities, she responded eagerly. All she needed was a date of birth and she could tell a person anything they needed to know. Likewise with Tarot, as soon as she touched a card, she received information.

I am not discounting or discrediting intuitive and natural psychic potential. But I must make it clear that gaining information by knowing someone's birthday or touching a Tarot card does not an astrologer or Tarotologist make! This student was obviously relying on her own natural psychic ability. Information received through intuitive means may be absolute and correct. But the knowledge of the birthday and the touching of a Tarot card has nothing to do with what such a person receives. This does not discount the importance and truth of the message. But it is not relative to the divinatory skills of a specific esoteric science.

Incidentally, this student is now a successful esoteric consultant. Her earlier story continued in this way. A person asked a question. The student eagerly volunteered to answer. "Just give me the date of your birth and choose a Tarot card," she said. The lady gave her date of birth and chose a Tarot card at random. Our student immediately gave a simple, general description of the lady's personality. Then her concentration went to the Tarot card and she repeatedly said how strongly she felt that something was about to happen. "It is good, very good," she repeated several times. The lady asked her anxiously what "it" was. "I don't know, but it's good," was the reply.

Here we had a clear demonstration of psychic ability. The astrological data was far too general and non-personal. A serious astrologer would have considered the information inadequate and dissatisfactory. The Tarotologist would have felt likewise.

The student herself could possibly have given more information had she recognized her psychic ability and developed her natural skills. Everyone has the same choice, to discover exactly where their esoteric skills are. If one has a natural psychic ability they can choose to develop the intuitive skills without combining a method of Divination. Alternatively, they could elect to study one of the esoteric sciences and use the additional boost of their natural intuitive powers.

So you should approach Psychic Development from your personal Point of Balance and a good basic understanding of the many choices available.

Basic Understanding of Choices

1. Recognize your own psychic potential.
2. Know that if it is not apparent, it can be discovered with a good reputable teacher.
3. Choose to develop your natural intuitive abilities.
4. Elect to study a form of Divination.
5. Understand clearly your source and how you are receiving information.
6. Learn how to combine your skills and achieve a level of competence in your chosen esoteric field.

CHAPTER SEVEN

CHOOSING YOUR ESOTERIC VOCATION

Your choice of esoteric vocation will be greatly influenced with your natural inclination. Discovering your own psychic tendencies will contribute toward your choice of subject. This book is intended to help the esoteric scholar formulate plans whereby they can experience the type of esoteric expression that stems from their incarnate desire.

A medical student must attend a specialized college to learn the essential facts relating to medicine and practice. Only after completing the preliminary requirements, and obtaining a level of competency, can he pursue a vocation and become a neurosurgeon or heart specialist, etc. It is the same with this work. The serious esoteric scholar must be taught the basic rudiments of Psychic Development.

Certain esoteric skills are quite complex and require concentrated study. Astrology, Tarotology and Gnothology are such skills. Each of these subjects requires an independent study of its own. If you have an interest in any such specialized area, you should acquire a proficient teacher. Begin by reading about the subject or making an appointment to discuss your interest with a knowledgeable person in that esoteric field.

Before any skill can be recognized, you must be prepared to learn everything you can about the subject. When you reach this stage, it is observed as being quite easy! To become fluent and knowledgeable in your subject puts you on the scholastic level. From this point your research becomes personal and your reputation is chiseled out of your personal effort and integrity.

ASTROLOGY

Astrology is much more than the horoscope in the newspaper. It all begins with your entrance into this world—the time, the date, the place. The complexity is absolutely fascinating. Everyone is born with an influence from one of the twelve signs of the zodiac. That is only the beginning! There are so many astrological procedures, each having its own separate section of information. In fact, after becoming an astrologer, you might continue your astrological career in any of the following special areas:

Natal astrology   Mundane astrology
Astrometeorology   Medical astrology
Predictive astrology   Inceptional astrology

I have not named all the possible outlets! The list goes on and each title preceding the "word" astrologer denotes yet another area of astrological expertise.

RECOGNITION WITHIN

I have indicated a need for long and arduous study when you consider the many esoteric sciences, but this is not meant to dissuade you. It is a sincere form of encouragement on my behalf, to allow the seeking student to see the wonderful areas of Psychic Development. Some of the esoteric sciences are more complex than others. This does not make one method of study and development any less valuable than another. There is a vast world of expression for Psychic Development. It is exciting and invigorating. It is also exacting and demanding, attracting the serious student to challenge the limitations of the normal and accepted level of Consciousness.

TAROT

This ancient esoteric science is practiced more today than at any other period in history. The reason, of course, is the wonderful availability and variety of Tarot cards. Here is an example of the old successfully merging with the new. In our day and age, the printing and distribution of Tarot cards has enabled the esoteric student to richly explore the mystical symbols of Tarotology.

One question I am asked repeatedly during my lecture tours and teaching is:

WHY ARE THE TAROT CARDS DIFFERENT? THERE ARE SO MANY TAROT DECKS, EACH SHOWING DIFFERENT PICTURES.

The answer is really quite simple. Each Tarot deck has a total of seventy-eight cards. Each of these cards is a symbol, like a musical note. Once you learn the interpretation of the symbol intellectually, then your intuitive energy is able to function and add further information. A competent Tarotologist, like a competent musician, is then able to give many renditions of his art.

The reason for the pictorial differences is the intuitive ability of the person who created the deck. Some Tarot experts have produced their own individual artwork to present their personal interpretation of each Tarot symbol. Dr. Arthur Edward Waite, who produced his deck in 1910, had the designs drawn and colored under his supervision by Pamela Coleman Smith, an American girl who was a fellow member of the occult society called "The Order of the Golden Dawn."

The Connolly deck was produced much in the same way. My son Peter Paul and I worked countless hours to create my personal interpretation of the mysterious Tarot symbols. The artwork by Peter Paul Connolly is breathtakingly beautiful. It was a long, slow procedure but the cards are an excellent and true visual picture of my personal interpretation of the symbology. Each of the pictures conveys to the Tarotologist the beauty, wisdom and esoteric translation of the mystical impressions received through the Higher Levels of Consciousness.

So the practicing Tarotologist has the opportunity, through his choice of deck, to share the vision of the originator. The choice of the

Tarotologist is governed by his own intuitive senses. He will select the Tarot deck according to how he can interpret the symbols most easily. As the Tarotologist learns to work with the symbols (cards) he must be able to tune into the mystical symbols and to do this he must first be attracted by the Conscious level.

My personal vision of esoteric images has been implanted in my Consciousness for many years, from the time when I was a very young woman. It was from that original energy form that I first began to write my series of handbooks. The esoteric pictures have never changed! Through the years, the colors and images just became more and more beautiful. I would sigh and wonder why all this had been given to *me*—I had no artistic ability. Yet these esoteric images were so magnificent. It didn't make any sense. I began to write my books wishing I could share so much more with my readers.

I married, and had some children, all quite talented. One day I was teaching my youngest son, Peter Paul, how to read. Suddenly I realized intuitively that this little boy, then age five, would be given the esoteric gift to portray my mystical pictures. I was so excited that I told him this with a huge amount of enthusiasm. So much so, he remembers it today! His older brother, Jonathan, and his sisters, Deborah, Catherine and Louise, all had artistic talent. I wondered why this gift could not have been given to one of them. Of course, karma plays a great part in this story and provides the answers.

I waited twenty years. During those years I deliberately avoided talking about what had happened. I didn't want Peter to grow up feeling my enthusiasm as a constant pressure. I certainly saw his artistic talent mature. He is a contemporary artist and I slowly felt the possibility disappearing. One day after twenty years, very simply, Peter Paul came to visit and announced that he was ready to work with me on the Connolly Tarot Deck.

The reason I share this true story is to encourage your studies and Psychic Development. If you know that you have something within you that is meant to be used or shared, keep your faith. When the time is ready, it will happen—it always does. Your intuitive ability is precious and should not be dominated by negative doubts. What is meant to be, will be. Follow the inner voice and pursue your esoteric goals with enthusiasm and a vigorous study program.

My own Tarot books,[3] like all my books, are written to help the esoteric student focus directly on the subject matter and also apply their intuitive abilities. There are many other excellent works by qualified authors. Go to the library and the bookstore. Browse and look seriously for what you need. Permit your Higher Self to inspire you. Enjoy the extensive selection of esoteric reading available. Once you feel the urge to go beyond your reading, then seek out a good esoteric learning program or teacher. Don't settle for anything less. There are many opportunities for learning available now for the esoteric scholar. Go and make inquiries and ask all the questions you need. A reputable establishment will welcome your enthusiasm.

GNOTHOLOGY

Gnothology is the science or study of the knowing within. It is a new term for the ancient Cabalistic study of numbers, which forms the roots of modern numerology (see *Connolly Book of Numbers*, vols. 1 and 2).

Here again, we have a specialized form of study—working with numbers and learning how to esoterically compute the information received. This knowledge is then used to define the possible pattern of personal activities, past, present and future.

Working with numbers and learning how to delineate a Gnothology chart is most rewarding. This type of Divination requires the ability to first work with numbers and numerical equations. Precision is necessary when composing the actual structure of the chart. The intuitive and esoteric skills are then used to interpret the numerical information, and the Gnothologist learns how to skillfully translate the final delineation through his intuitive expertise.

Gnothology is much like astrology when we consider the many possible aspects of expression. A chart may be basic, or specifically

---

[3] See *Tarot, A New Handbook for the Apprentice*, vol. 1, and *Tarot, The Handbook for the Journeyman*, vol. 2.

structured to extract certain information. A complete chart is versatile and flexible, and the Gnothologist can extract pertinent information about karma.

There are many other aspects of Gnothology entailing personality, health and inherent qualities. The source, which is Cabalistic, is a learning procedure that is ancient and deeply complex. The final interpretation is extracted from the source and translated according to the nature or type of Divination used, such as astrology, Gnothology or Tarotology.

THE CABALISTIC ROOTS

From the mystical concept of the Cabala we find other possible divinatory expressions. The wisdom of the Cabala has been explored by the Masters throughout time. These particular "ologies," such as Gnothology, are really extracts from the Tree of Life—each is a Branch of Learning.

The Cabala is recognized as the Tree of Life. Imagine your own family tree. How far back does it go? Whether or not you have the actual data or records, it is exciting to realize that it goes back—*you* go back—to the very beginning! The Cabalistic Tree of Life also goes back to the beginning. Many seeds of esoteric procedure and discipline have taken strong roots. They have been cultivated and encouraged to grow in such ways that it is difficult sometimes for the expert to recognize the original structure.

Even with my lifelong study, I cannot possibly conceive that I will ever, in this one life, discover everything I need to know. The seasons of the Tree of Life have been affected by the growth and seasons of man. Down through the centuries, wisdom has been passed on. The Cabalistic scholar has had limited access to the written word. Normally this scholar has to be taught by word-of-mouth to comprehend the mysterious workings and wisdom of the Tree of Life.

Each "ology," then, emerged as a new growth, and we now have astrology, Gnothology and Tarotology. The Tree of Life is like any other tree that grows and has the ability to reproduce itself and propagate a new growth. To interpret the language of the mysical Tree of Life, one has to learn the symbolic Cabalistic language. The intuitive powers of man contribute toward the mystery of the Cabala. This magnificent union of intellect and intuition is the secret of life itself.

It is important to understand that the complexity of symbolism contained within the structure of the Tree of Life provides the substance or basic root theories from which many Divination procedures derived their original inheritance.

VIA MYSTICA

The Latin words for the Mystic Path are *Via Mystica*. It is said that when the student is ready, the Master appears. At what time in the student's search does this happen? It happens when the student has honestly decided to walk the *Via Mystica*. You may very well be upon the *Via Mystica*! All roads have a beginning and an end. Our next question may be, "Who determines the beginning and the end?" We can do this ourselves by recognizing where we start!

Many are attracted to beginning at the end. They take a flight of fancy and desire, and then begin their personal journey back to the rudiments or basic concepts, which must be fully understood before arriving at the journey's end. So, whichever way you begin your journey will inevitably produce one experience at the beginning of *Via Mystica* and two possible ends! Regardless of *how* you take this spiritual journey, like a sandwich, the meat is in the center.

If you approach the *Via Mystica* correctly, before you is the insatiable esoteric appetite. As you experience the mysteries of esoteric phenomenon, you are satisfying your appetite and therefore enjoying the intake of knowledge. If and when you have satisfied this hunger, you reach a level of spiritual satisfaction. A transition of comprehension transpires and then, lo! and behold, looming before you is yet another *Via Mystica*!

The path of the esoteric student is never-ending. Hopefully, we retain the knowledge gained and continue with no backtracking as we go from one life experience to another. For surely the *Via Mystica* has to be the spiritual path back to God? If we can look at our spiritual ventures this way, we will have little or no difficulty in realizing that wisdom never changes; only the human concept changes. The karmic path of destiny leads us all to the *Via Mystica*.

When the esoteric scholar accepts his life experience as the *key* to his karmic path, then he will be privileged to remove his worn shoes of trial and error and walk the *Via Mystica* in joy and anticipation. Psychic Development is a part of this whole process when the esoteric senses are alert—not only to the ability of application, but also to the responsibility of use. Then the process of development will be expanded to many areas of esoteric expression.

The goal of all esoteric scholars should be to walk the *Via Mystica*, to be ever-ready for the mystical union of scholar and teacher. The ego is folded and neither scholar nor teacher is recognized, for they wear the same gown of spirituality. These esoteric thoughts may seem vague but to the true scholar they are a Cabalistic key that will enable you to start your spiritual journey on the *Via Mystica*.

CHAPTER EIGHT

GNOTHI SEAUTON

Translated, *Gnothi Seauton* means "Know thyself." Have you experienced difficulty in establishing relationships? If so, this next step could be the reason why. Think for a moment how the mind sometimes works. It's here, then it's there, in a flash. It doesn't appear to bring anything back after it has explored a million things. Usually this can be considered a way of relaxing or unwinding after a dose of hard work or concentration. Arriving home from work, we kick off our shoes, turn on the television, make the coffee and begin to open the mail. Before all this activity has registered, the phone rings, the kettle boils, the dog is trying to read your mail and all at once the television is too loud.

Sounds like bedlam, doesn't it? That's exactly what it is. A far more soothing procedure is organized relaxation. It is seldom used. Stealing a few minutes of peace is not always the answer. Nerves remain frayed and you eventually go to bed fully exhausted. Let's start again. Begin by remembering the keyword, *Gnothi Seauton*, Know Thyself.

POWER OF CH'I

Sometimes it seems almost impossible to relax. Even when everything appears conducive to relaxation, it is not always easy to discontinue physical and mental activity. The secret is the Ch'i, or life energy, that flows within the physical body. The power of Ch'i is considered the core of Universal Energy. As a spiritual practice, you tune into this vital energy and your physical body begins to move in unison with the Universal flow. During this spiritual activity, the physical body appears to be dancing, as the student endeavors to blend with the rhythm of the Universal Energies.

You don't have to be an expert at this to derive spiritual benefits. A mother holds her baby close and moves in gentle rhythm to rock the child to sleep. This is an inherent ability of the mother to adapt herself to the Ch'i of her child. Have you noticed how, at first, a baby will react and reject the mother's efforts to console? But when the mother gently persists to reach the Ch'i of her infant, very soon they are melded in perfect Universal harmony. Looking at a flower and observing its color and beauty can also arouse your inner urge to harmonize.

There is a natural force within us all that urges us to blend with the Universal Energies. A walk on the beach or being in any special place can stimulate this natural instinct. The urge or instinct should never be dismissed. Each time you avail yourself of your own Ch'i, and release it to the incoming flow of the Universe, you will be refreshed in body and mind.

If you make a conscious effort to allow the input of the Universal flow to penetrate and enter every pore of your body, you will ensure a pure stream of Ch'i. At that moment you will feel no longer alone. You will be spiritually transformed and become One with every living thing. From this special strength you will realize the true meaning of *Gnothi Seauton*.

EXERCISE 5: TOUCHING THE CH'I

This gentle, yet exhilarating, esoteric exercise eliminates stagnant negativity. The vibrancy of this energy can penetrate any and all resisting factors. As the physical body breathes in oxygen, the etheric body thrives on the spiritual substance contained in the Universal Force.

Dress lightly and loosely so you can move about easily. Have sufficient space around you. Remove any jewelry that may inhibit your movement or distract you. Do not wear shoes or slippers. You can have bare feet or good-fitting socks.

You can play background music as long as it has soothing melodic tones, but play it softly because your sensitivity can develop quickly using this exercise. Some students who are developing intuitively often experience clairaudient sounds during this exercise.

Start by sitting in a comfortable chair and begin to relax as much as you can, physically and mentally.

The target of your spiritual focus begins by separating your Conscious level from the actual esoteric process. This enables you to obtain the full benefit of an exercise. By preparing everything correctly, you can be assured that you will receive and gain a new spiritual insight, as you learn to leave the weight of your Conscious level behind. Each time you return to this level of Consciousness, you will find it has relaxed and gained a new strength entirely from your spiritual endeavors.

1. Relaxing, close your eyes and visualize drawing back deeply within yourself.
   (Wait.)

2. Sense the darkness around you. Move slowly toward a small bright light in the center of your being.
   (Wait.)

3. As you come in closer to the small bright light it appears to be like a star. Shooting rays of SILVER energy extend out into the darkness.
   (Wait.)

4. As you continue to come closer, feel a pull of energy and the desire to merge directly into the bright star.
   (Wait.)

5. Know that in the center of the star is your personal source of Ch'i. Now feel your strength building and press forward toward the bright light.
   (Wait.)

6. Pause now to listen very carefully. What do you hear? Sense the change of vibrations and listen.
   (Wait.)

7. Facing the bright light of your personal Star of Ch'i, feel the vibratory force on your face and body.
(Wait.)

8. The star now is extending bright WHITE rays. Feel them touching your face, body, hands and hair. Enjoy this wonderful sensation of rejuvenation.
(Wait.)

9. It is easy now to move forward. As you make your next step, the center of the bright star opens and pure GOLD rays of light burst forth. Golden threads are now spinning around your body. It is a beautiful feeling.
(Wait.)

10. Now, completely coiled in the Golden energy, lift UP, UP, UP. You are moving swiftly and the Golden threads begin unwinding as you journey UP and above your Conscious level.
(Wait.)

11. You are totally free. The GOLD threads are now behind you. The power that moves you is healing your physical body and you feel exhilarated with your spiritual vision.
(Wait.)

12. You can see many things. If you listen carefully you can also hear music and voices.
(Wait.)

13. Move your arms and legs and feel the vibratory force of Ch'i surging through every atom of your being. It is the Life Force and you can extract all you need just by thought alone.
(Wait.)

14. You have never known such love and protection. Look at your body and see how it vibrates in the power of Ch'i. See how quickly it moves. Each place the Light touches fills your soul with purity and love.
(Wait.)

15. Enjoy the movement, enjoy the vibrancy, and feel the freedom of your soul.
(Wait.)

16. Now look below and see your physical body surrounded with the same bright light. Watch the light as it enters your body. See how the gray negative energy slowly drains away. (Wait.)

17. It is time now to come back to the Conscious level. You are moving swiftly once again. Your body is before you. Step immediately into the physical body. As you feel your body around you stretch your arms and legs. As you do this the energy spreads rapidly and fills the physical body with its new vibrant power. Feel the Ch'i energy as it travels to every part of your body. (Wait.)

18. Give thanks for this spiritual experience. Ask that you might contain this Universal Force, and use it well to improve every aspect of your life. (Wait.)

19. Take three deep, easy breaths and, as you expel the breath, feel the new control and power that you now have. Your body is full of Light. You have touched the Ch'i. Health and prosperity are waiting. Put them into your life. (Wait.)

20. Open your eyes and gently move your physical body. Stretch like a cat and allow the Ch'i to extend to every cell within the body. You have touched the Life-giving Force of Ch'i. You are in command. You have extracted power from the Universe. Use it well and always be aware of the Life Force within.

CHAPTER NINE

THE ESOTERIC THREAD

Life is a huge, magnificent pattern of our personal activity. Life is not fragments of experience that happen by themselves. Everything that we are is being created by us every day that we live. The pattern of your activity can be changed. All you need is an Esoteric thread of personal stamina and strength. This thread is found in the Soul Center.

Refuse to allow fear within, and nothing on the outside will harm you. If we come from a point of inner contentment, we are immediately fortified with a special power that will pull us through any remaining obstacles. This simplicity of joy is the answer. Forget the usual things that bring you to this peak. Start looking at the real issues in life. Happiness, I guarantee, supercedes all ambition. Perhaps you feel it takes specific things to make you happy. Maybe these things do make you happy, but they should not *control* your personal joy and happiness.

Focus on inner joy and happiness and you will see your life in a different way. Looking at life from a point of joy changes absolutely everything! It is so simple, yet so effective. If you do this enough, you will probably conjure up enough energy to laugh at yourself. The energy spent worrying about what we don't have should be salvaged and used as a fortress of strength, opposing and refusing to allow any negativity to inundate your Soul Center.

Find new areas of genuine concern to occupy your thoughts. Like attracts like. If you are unafraid and joy radiates from your soul you will undoubtedly attract all the situations you have been yearning for. To invest time and worry on things you cannot change is a waste of energy. The very second you focus on *inner* joy you will feel the strength and security of the Life-giving Force.

All this may raise some questions in your mind:

1. What is the Esoteric Thread?

2. How do I use it in my life?

3. Will the Esoteric Thread help my Psychic Development?

These are indeed important questions. The answers can change everything!

WHAT IS THE ESOTERIC THREAD?

The Esoteric Thread is a vibratory force that coils around and solidifies into a tiny golden ball. In this form, it is easily manipulated and bounces back and forth within the Emotional level. The Emotional level is activated by the balance or imbalance of the emotions. Governed by the Conscious level, the golden ball has no particular direction. Each emotion sharply moves the ball. This vibratory action causes instability, lack of control, fear and upset.

The small golden ball is actually changed in color and size by emotional activity. Each time you decide to make a fresh start, the ball is reduced and reflects the gold vibrations of the coiled Esoteric Thread. When you lose control, the golden ball changes color, and if you maintain a level of negativity, the ball increases in size.

The Emotional level, or "E" level, is located just above the natural waistline, directly under the rib cage. In moments of panic or fear, you feel a lurch as the solidified ball moves in response to fear. If you have been in a negative state for a long period of time then you are affected physically in that area of your body.

The complexity of the Emotional level is strongly related to the chakra system, which indicates the esoteric condition of the Etheric body (see *Karma Without Stress*). This physical area of the body needs the constant input of natural vibratory flow. The small golden ball is a natural phenomenon. Problems occur through lack of knowledge. This esoteric level is usually ignored.

In its correct condition, the tiny "ball" should be clear and bright gold. It is a coil of Esoteric Thread that contains its own unique mystical properties. Any emotional activity that does not stem from self-control or a state of joy causes uncomfortable movement of the ball. The ball adheres to negative input and loses its power as it is slowly wrapped around and around with the tone and nature of the negative flow.

The apparent sensitivity of the gold ball is really a demonstration of its power and purpose! In its original state it is bright and about half an inch in diameter. As you allow attacking negativity to flood the "E" level, the esoteric coil which is the golden ball immediately responds, to protect and defend. In doing so, it absorbs the unwanted energies and seemingly submits to the undesired emotions.

Actually, it is forced to repulse the unwanted negativity and in the process of rejecting, it absorbs and increases in size. Until the Conscious level begins to relax, the gold coil is trapped and engorged with the undesirable influence.

The coil transforms according to the type of negativity. It can be seen easily by a clairvoyant. In fact, I have known several situations where a clairvoyant did not understand what they were seeing! A natural medium interprets what they see. If they have not been exposed to esoteric philosophic teachings, then it is virtually impossible to expect an esoteric translation. Consequently, a vivid-red, moving ball of energy was interpreted as a positive sign by one clairvoyant. This oversized red energy represented a terribly angry person. Incidentally, the angry person had told the clairvoyant exactly how he felt. The clairvoyant was not wrong in what she saw, but through lack of esoteric knowledge, she misinterpreted what she saw.

If any part of the Etheric structure is directly affected, then the coil reflects the type of energy causing the problem. The Conscious mind determines this activity with its constant focus. If, for example, you used the Higher Consciousness instead, and applied the same amount of energy, life as you know it would completely change. You would live in a state of joy. This joy would be a result of the emotional activity being monitored and controlled. The basic Conscious level can project images of fear so real that it is actually frightening. Similarly, if we do this, or we don't do that, we "know" exactly what will happen! This is because we have trained ourselves to envision negative possibilities. Therefore, to discover and come in touch with the Esoteric Thread, we have to bypass the Conscious level.

We can achieve this by using Exercise 6, which redirects your normal focus to the Golden Coil. My students have had rapid and outstanding results using the Golden Coil exercise. Physical conditions are also affected working with this exercise. The health improves and, instead of trying to change attitudes, the different vibratory flow releases at such a depth that there is an immediate sense of well-being.

EXERCISE 6: THE GOLDEN COIL

Lie down and take the time to relax. A GOLD or YELLOW candle helps considerably. You do not need music, as your concentration may be affected. Make sure you have disconnected the telephone and that your pet will not disturb you. Dress loosely and lightly, with no uncomfortable jewelry.

Remember that this beautiful exercise will accelerate your Psychic Development. Gaining inner control is a huge step and will increase your psychic energy.

1. Put your concentration on your Inner Eye. This is located at the top of the nose, between the eyebrows.
   (Wait.)

2. Allow the warmth of INDIGO to pulsate gently in the area of your Inner Eye, and feel the comfort of INDIGO spread.
   (Wait.)

3. Completely relax and hold the INDIGO. Focus in the very center of the color and wait until you see a small WHITE energy there.
   (Wait.)

4. From the top of your head, the Crown center, look down to the WHITE energy surrounded by the soft warm INDIGO. (Wait.)

5. Inhale a slow, easy breath, imagining that it flows in through the top of your head. Release it gently down to the Inner Eye, and then slowly push the WHITE energy down into the Throat. Do this again, slowly and easily pushing the WHITE energy down into the Throat. Continue to breathe in this way until the WHITE light is stabilized. (Wait.)

6. Now you are ready to go deeper. Breathe in through the top of the head and, as you release the breath, push the WHITE light down to the Heart. As the energy touches your Heart center, feel the light extend as it becomes stabilized in this area. (Wait.)

7. Reach up to the top of your head and feel the control of the Crown center. Breathe easily and look down to your Throat center and see the WHITE light pulsating there. (Wait.)

8. Again, look down from the Crown, the control center. Remaining relaxed and breathing naturally and easily, look down to your Heart center. See the WHITE light pulsating in rhythm with your Heart center. (Wait.)

9. Reaching up again to your control center at the Crown, take a slow, deep easy breath and release it straight through the Throat center, through the Heart center, and into the Emotional level. Continue to breathe this way until you stabilize the WHITE light. (Wait.)

10. When the light is stabilized, go up once again to the Crown center and feel yourself being energized with a brilliant powerful energy. Feel it rush through your body. See yourself completely absorbed in the brilliant light. Feel the power rushing

through. You are being prepared. You are receiving energy from the Universal Force.
(Wait.)

11. All aspects of Consciousness are going to merge. When you next release your breath, you will do so with a strong force. The power that now surrounds you at the Crown center floods the Emotional level with its light. You are now going to inhale a deep, easy slow breath. Hold it for a count of three and then release it quickly to the Emotional level. You are now focused onthe Emotional level. With the light that surrounds you, look and see what is taking place there. See any emotional pockets filled with negativity.
(Wait.)

12. Your spiritual quest is to find the Golden Coil. If there is negativity, you will recognize it only as a ball of colored energy. Look for this ball, to see where it is hidden. When you see a glow of color other than WHITE you will know that you are near the ball. Now find it.
(Wait.)

13. Notice the color(s). Remember the size of the ball. Inhale deeply the strong WHITE light that is around you. Know that you are responsible for any turmoil or fear. See yourself standing straight and lifting your arms up into the light. Call for the angel Raphael. You will feel his presence as a cool breeze. When he appears, ask how you may retrieve your Golden Coil. He will speak and direct you. Listen well and follow His holy guidance. You will find the Golden Coil quite easily. Listen to the wisdom of the angel Raphael. You will bring back your Golden Coil in total joy and then continue with your spiritual quest.
(Wait at least five minutes.)

14. It is time now to continue your journey. The Golden Coil is in your hands. Now you must take this spiritual treasure to the light and power of the Crown chakra. Inhale a deep breath and go up to your Heart center. See and feel the light of the Heart center fuse with the power in your Golden Coil. As the ener-

gies merge, be aware of the sacred path you now take.
(Wait.)
Then follow this same procedure for the Throat center.
(Wait.)

15. Inhale once again and swiftly go up to the Inner Eye. See and feel the light of the Inner Eye. The magnificent forces meld together and you can feel the power as it glows and radiates all around you—flashes of INDIGO and GOLD. A rush and exhilaration of pure untouched energy—your whole body is reacting with the Universal Force. Everything is changing. Your life path is now clear and open before you. Look at your future, and see what you must do to bring peace and harmony into your life.
(Wait.)

16. Holding the Golden Coil, you are now ready to go up into the wisdom and power of the Crown chakra. Slowly you begin to rise. Feel the heat of the brilliant light above your head. As you rise into the beauty and glory of the Crown chakra, lift up your Golden Coil and envision everything becoming GOLD around you. This golden energy will reinforce your determination. It is giving you all you need to walk on your true karmic path. As you reach the center of your Crown chakra, let go of the Golden Coil. Look down and see it move like an arrow down through the Inner Eye, through the Throat center, through the Heart center and into its rightful place. Your Emotional level now extends rays of power to every part of your body, mind and spirit.
   Now spend a few moments and give thanks.

HOW DO I USE THE ESOTERIC THREAD IN MY LIFE?

The Esoteric Thread is a pure vibratory cord of gold. This cord is composed of thoughts, words and deeds that are relevant to the continuing Psychic Development of your Higher Self. It is woven from the moral fibers and it naturally forms into the Golden Coil.

The ancient Masters recognized the power of spiritual control. One of the first duties of the new esoteric student was to find the Golden Coil and remove any negative energies that had formed. The spiritual quest was a lonely path, as the beginning student had the difficult task of first locating the Golden Coil.

The Golden Coil Exercise, above, helps you discover and purify your Golden Coil. This esoteric cleansing procedure may have to be done frequently to ensure that the coil is on its true level. Only when the coil is in a state of spiritual perfection can you begin to manifest the Esoteric Thread.

The Esoteric Thread is a composition of thoughts, words and deeds.

Thoughts

Making a determined effort to think good things is a good place to begin. It's not so easy—when negativity starts flowing, it is difficult to stop. But thank goodness, it is not impossible! As you soon as you become aware that you are permitting a negative flow of thoughts to enter your Consciousness, *stop* right there and then! The moment you apply this kind of spiritual discipline, you are creating the Esoteric Thread that will instantly wrap around the Golden Coil. Even though a fraction of negativity happened and entered your Consciousness, the mere act of applying discipline instigates the energy needed to manufacture the Esoteric Thread. This, in turn, adheres itself to your Golden Coil and wraps around it.

Words

"Think before you speak" is the simple answer to managing words. If you fail to do this, and then realize what you are saying, *stop* and change the manner of your conversation. Words are like weapons and they can destroy you or harm some undeserving soul. A mere suggestion can inflame someone else to carry the torch you yourself lighted!

If you have gone too far in the conversation and cannot repair what you have done, inhale a deep White breath, and whatever it takes to correct it, *do so*. Admit, if necessary, that you were being unduly critical or unkind. Perhaps you were not thinking straight, or maybe you derived some pleasure or satisfaction in seeing the reaction of what you had to say. Whatever your reason, it doesn't matter. What does matter is that you extract the strength you need to correct it immediately.

It won't be as difficult as you think! For when you make that spiritual decision to correct something, then a wonderful phenomenon takes place. The Higher Self comes to the rescue, and the Esoteric Thread is spun rapidly around your Golden Coil. As this wonderful energy is manifest, you derive a great measure of internal strength— and the trauma is nullified.

The Esoteric Thread is also activated when you are listening to the words spoken by others. If you feel angry or disturbed as you hear certain things being said, take a deep breath, inhaling White Light, and then visualize the actual words spoken being showered with your outgoing breath. Again, this esoteric procedure initiates an immediate response from "E" level. The Esoteric Thread is made possible by your refusal to accept the anger or hurt on your "E" level. The outward and physical act of releasing your breath, and using it to cancel the potential input of negativity, promptly causes the Golden Coil to be protected by the Esoteric Thread.

Deeds

Negative actions require an entirely different approach. Rather than try to repair an act, which could be difficult to do, we use the prevention method. When you accept that the other points of esoteric concern—your thoughts and words—are on constant alert, then it will be hardly likely for you to indulge in negative deeds.

Begin each day recognizing your responsibility for your thoughts, words and deeds. Inhale White Light and, as you exhale, visualize your outgoing breath as a shower over the whole day ahead. Know that when you encounter negativity in others, you have the unique opportunity of protecting yourself by manifesting the Esoteric Thread.

A SIMPLE WAY TO START YOUR DAY

I ask that my THOUGHTS be pure and clear,
I ask for WORDS not spoken in fear.
I pray that my DEEDS, my needs won't spoil,
My gift will be THREAD for my GOLDEN COIL.

WILL THE ESOTERIC THREAD HELP MY PSYCHIC DEVELOPMENT?

You now know what the Esoteric Thread is and how it is created. You also know the ancient secret of where it is located. You have the simple prayer to start each new day. Now, the third question is whether the Esoteric Thread will help your Psychic Development.

The answer, of course, is very definitely "yes." You have learned to touch the Ch'i, and you know the mysterious workings of the Golden Coil. At this point of your esoteric journey you are well-prepared to travel your karmic path of destiny.

Of course, you will encounter difficulty—one always does. But as long as you cling to your basic knowledge, you can travel competently along your karmic path of destiny. It is this basic esoteric knowledge that will open bright new vistas of opportunity. Your Psychic Development has to have a good solid foundation. These preliminary procedures are an essential part of its foundation. Learn and practice them well. Put yourself in a state of "readiness" at all times. Be open to new thought-streams as your Consciousness develops and your spiritual ability improves. Have patience with yourself and make strong immovable goals.

You are now ready to explore your inherent powers. With your present knowledge, you can encourage more growth and satisfaction for yourself. There are no quick routes to success, be it spiritual or material. Do things right, and the right things will happen. Enjoy the strength of your newfound knowledge. At last, you can consider yourself a true esoteric scholar, for you are now prepared to venture forward, and yet you are not afraid to go back to your basics.

There is so much to learn, and the way of the esoteric scholar is one of light and joy. This light and joy is not limited. It stretches out to all exciting possibilities. What lies before you? What comes next? The most wonderful and exciting adventure of *life*. Your life! Maybe you have a few things to tidy up here and there. But remember, you now know how, and that is going to be your motivating force.

The Esoteric Thread is absolutely an essential part of your Psychic Development. As the sun rises and you begin your day, first recognize the God energies waiting to be used within you. As the sun sets and your day ends, give thanks for the Life-giving Force that surges through your body, mind and soul. All this will help your esoteric growth. Know and understand your purpose. Acknowledge the source of love and life. Reach out and expand your Consciousness. Doing all these things will provide an excellent foundation. The Esoteric Thread will wind around the Golden Coil as you make your progress. Without it, we remain locked in our physical and material concerns. It is the moral fiber of success on all levels. Those who are aware of the Esoteric Thread, and are intent on spiritual progress, attract all earthly joys. The mysterious workings of the Esoteric Thread will become an inseparable part of your Psychic Development.

THE CROSSROADS

The first Tarot card of the Major Arcana is the FOOL. We see him standing at the Crossroads, deciding which path to take. I'm sure you have had that feeling many times. We may not be sure which path to take, and we must take the time to consider the alternatives. This is part of your Psychic Development.

Once you have practiced the esoteric exercises, your mind will be much clearer. Your vision will be extended and you will be busy putting things in order. Without committing yourself in any direction, at least permit yourself to evaluate the choices before you. It is too easy to fall back into the pattern of acceptance. Even if you are having reasonable success in a present activity, this does not prohibit you from exploring other possibilities. Also, you must avoid remaining as you are because it seems more comfortable.

This brings us back to the Crossroads—your Crossroads and your choices. One sure way of limiting your choices is by not acknowledging that they exist. How often have you arrived at the conclusion that you don't have any choice? The truth is, we always have a choice. We just become reluctant to exercise that choice because we anticipate a series of undesirable events. One could even argue that this is reasonable. But it's important to see matters clearly and completely. If we look at a situation and we are not equipped with all the details, we can miss out sorely on opportunity.

OPPORTUNITY

Opportunity is not likely to jump out and say "Here I am," if you take no chances. If you walk the same familiar path, the well-worn path of boredom and certainty, you will miss opportunities. Opportunity offers a new way of expressing *you*. It might require an effort to do this, since you are not quite sure how you will perform. At least, that's what you think and feel. The truth is, you already know all these things. When you are confronted with choice, deep down inside you know what you should do. The trouble and confusion starts when you avoid the inner wisdom. You dance around the opportunity and, in doing so, you smother the power you have, by presenting yourself with one excuse after another.

Sometimes people are forced to take the opportunities that life offers. Translated, this means only that you were forced to make a decision. After you made the decision, you adapted as quickly as you could, and made the best of it. Usually the results are fondly spoken of as "luck." Don't you feel a little sad when you realize how many times you have denied yourself a new opportunity? The world, your world, is brimming with opportunity. You may have to look hard and broaden your vision, but nevertheless, your world is full of opportunity. Have you ever thought of how you look at opportunity?

CHAPTER TEN

ESOTERIC CONTROL

The Esoteric Control System has a chain of command throughout the physical body. In this series of books you will be learning more relating to the command capacity. The controlling energy may be considered neutral, dormant or even nonexistent, unless it is generated and exercised. In the same way, an inactive limb will begin to deteriorate if it is not used.

Imagine having a closet full of tools but not knowing where the key is! You continue to find other means of working without the correct tools. Eventually you achieve a good level of craftsmanship and forget the fine tools still locked away. This is like the powerful energy that is locked within your Consciousness.

The power within the Esoteric Control System has a tremendous capacity to open up areas of thought and creativity hitherto unknown. Just think of all our self-imposed limitations—the blockages that are nourished by lack of belief and not using our inner wisdom. You are much more powerful than you may be ready to believe.

SELF-HEALING ABILITY

The Conscious mind works from what it knows. It has a limited capacity of esoteric comprehension. More and more, each day we read and hear how the mind is capable of rendering healing to the physical body. This is not a revelation—it has been practiced since time began. In your Esoteric Control System is the power to heal the physical body. What is really interesting is that there are so many ways in which the physical body can be rejuvenated and healed.

Healing through the Esoteric Control System requires the cooperation of the mind on a Conscious level. This perhaps causes a problem —it is not easy to use the Conscious level for esoteric purposes. This is because the mind has difficulty focusing for long periods. The Conscious mind is always on guard, and it reacts and alerts the body when certain situations and messages are registered. Meditation can draw the Conscious mind away from its normal security position in the brain. Once the mind recognizes it can rest and still react to any incoming vibrations, it allows the door to the Higher Consciousness to open.

The Esoteric Control System is fed through the Crown chakra. This is at the center top of the head. There is a pure flow of Universal Energy that enters freely and fills the actual chakra area. Since the day of birth there has been a constant, steady vibratory flow which gradually takes this energy directly to the brain.

The brain and the nervous system are connected with the immune system. This suggests that a direct route of healing is readily available. The actual power to self-heal resides in every human being. This incredible power is not a ghost-like substance, it is an actual living force that allows the capacity to heal. You may wonder why it isn't the talk of the town! Why isn't it in this morning's headlines?

The physical brain has always been a fascinating subject. We are continually amazed at what doctors' research reveals. Today, many doctors are acknowledging man's power to heal. No one knows for sure exactly how it works, but evidence has already been presented for the self-healing capability.

The Esoteric Control System is governed by Conscious thought. It works very much like any other part of the physical body. If you clench your fist, it will remain that way until your brain receives the impulse to release the fingers. Fortunately, we have learned to control the physical body to some extent, and we don't give the signal controls much thought, do we?

An outstanding athlete who achieves extraordinary power makes everyone wish they had the same ability. The athlete, like the ballerina, like the man next door, extracts exactly what he needs. And so do you! Let's look further into the wonderful possibility of extracting even more from the Esoteric Control System.

The brain is responsive to the activity of the mind. If, for example, we firmly believe we are going to be sick, we soon start recognizing the symptoms. Yet a reverse thought pattern can induce healthy vibrations. This very fine line of mental decision governs the status of our health. The mental dilemma is that we expect to become old, we expect to become sick—and we do.

HEAL THYSELF

There is another part of you that is as important and real as you are. This is your Higher Self. The Higher Self is seldom recognized or known. It is not involved with or protected by your ego. Remaining firm and secure, it endeavors to influence your daily Conscious thoughts. Unfortunately, the Higher Self does not receive the appreciation it deserves. This is strange, since this powerful aspect of our existence is with us at all times. In dire cases of extreme emergency, when the Conscious mind loses its control, the Higher Self is there to support and protect. Our study is going to show you how you can begin immediately to familiarize yourself with your Higher Self.

THE HIGHER SELF

The power of the Higher Self is the true source of Psychic Development. There are many ways in which you can avail yourself of this power. One, of course, is the ability to apply self-healing. This healing power is not limited to physical healing. The vibratory qualities emanating from the Higher Self can induce healing on any level, thus providing the essential esoteric needs to accelerate Psychic Development.

So this is where you begin, with "self," looking within, and examining your own exciting potential. It all starts by recognizing that you are far greater than your reflection in the mirror. Surrounded by your own spiritual abilities, you can learn how to use your esoteric skills and how to recognize the many choices of esoteric expression available. A medical doctor knows more about your physical structure than you do. Even though *you* exist within your body, a doctor can usually examine you and determine what is happening better than you could. In the same way, you can learn how to analyze your own psychic powers, by electing to explore the many avenues of esoteric expression.

Becoming aware of your innate, latent skill begins with a sense of "coming in." By this, I mean you must learn to spend periods of time cut off from your normal everyday behavior and activities. Allowing yourself a predetermined allotment of time gives the Conscious level exactly what it needs—a sense of control. (Remember, the Conscious level is reluctant to let go.) If you determine that you are going to spend time studying, then the Conscious mind will respond by relaxing somewhat. This permits the Higher Self to communicate without undue interference.

Your Higher Self is the part of you that contains all the knowledge of your existence. Your Higher Self has always existed! In all past-life possibilities, the Higher Self remains unchanged. This, then, tells you that the "perfected you" has always existed. Each life experience is accompanied by the Higher Self. It is the part of you that is not severed from the divine source. It is constantly replenished from this source, while the Conscious level is extracting whatever *it* needs, and depleting the vibratory flow.

When your psychic ability and intuitive powers are working, you are, in fact, communicating with or through your Higher Self. There is absolutely nothing to prevent you from using this ability. In an emergency, you use it automatically; when the Conscious level is unable to cope with a situation, it opens up and allows a thrust of esoteric power, enabling it to act with precision and power.

GAINING ACCESS TO THE HIGHER SELF

Access to the Higher Self begins by acknowledgement. Knowing that you are a part of the Universal Force is sufficient to fulfill this requirement. You have a vital spiritual connection with the Universal Force, and this is through the Higher Self. Your first step is to acknowledge your Higher Self—a unique but simple step to take.

COMING IN

Connecting with your Higher Self is essentially an internal process. The discovery of this phenomenon is made within yourself. The spiritual quest to locate your Higher Self occurs deep within the Heart chakra. It is from this esoteric point that you can find the Missing Link.

Before you attempt to use the exercise "Merging with the Higher Self," it would be a good idea to let the Conscious level help you. Do this by practicing and experimenting with the following exercise, "Acquiring Esoteric Control." This exercise is a Conscious effort to reach and experience a higher level of sensitivity—to broaden and expand your regular Conscious experience. We begin with a flower or leaf as a focal point. The Conscious level has the ability to associate natural beauty with an unexplored esoteric source. There is a bridge between the two levels that the beginning student can cross quite easily.

Then the exercise to merge with the Higher Self can be used on inanimate objects, the purpose being to learn the rudiments of manifestation, a method whereby one can escalate the esoteric process and develop the psychic ability to intensify the vibratory structure of affirmations.

EXERCISE 7: ACQUIRING ESOTERIC CONTROL

Normally when you look at a flower, you would admire color, shape and beauty. Your energies would be flowing out toward the flower. The response of what you saw would then create a vibratory pattern of sensation. This would, in turn, cause your Emotional level to respond accordingly.

Imagine your eyes seeing the flower. The results of the vision go immediately to the Emotional level. Your "E" level responds and you have consciously enjoyed looking at a flower.

But you can go beyond that usual procedure by exercising Esoteric Control, and initiate a different response! You can extend your sensitivity beyond the physical and Conscious levels. By using this exercise you can learn how to change the normal Conscious approach and replace it with an esoteric approach.

1. Sit comfortably and place a flower or leaf before you on a table.

2. Sit as close to the table as possible so you are in close physical contact.

3. Be very relaxed and look at the flower easily. This doesn't require an intensive staring or concentration.

4. As you observe the flower, hold the vision, then close your eyes. Inhale deeply, slowly and easily. Bring in the physical vision of the flower directly through the center of your Emotional level. Then visualize the flower and the incoming breath going up directly to the center of the Heart chakra.

5. Hold the vision of the flower and the incoming breath in the center of the Heart chakra. As you begin to release your breath, feel a GOLDEN shower of vibrations falling away from your physical body. At the same time feel the flower swell and grow in the Heart center. As it does, it becomes more and more beautiful.

6. Continue your breathing procedure, inhaling the physical vision of the flower through the Emotional level and up to the center of the Heart chakra. Release the breath easily and feel the flower expand in beauty, color and radiance. As the flower expands within the Heart center, the outgoing breath creates a golden shower falling away from your physical body.

7. When the flower increases in size and beauty and fills the entire Heart chakra, then go up to the Inner Eye in one quick short breath. Release the breath from the Inner Eye back to the Heart chakra in a forcible golden shower.

8. Now be still, soul-still. Go into the golden shower, into the Heart center, and touch the flower. Breathe normally and begin inhaling the exquisite perfume of the flower.

9. As you smell the fragrance, descend slowly to the center of the Emotional level. Take a deep WHITE energy breath. Release the outgoing breath as a WHITE powerful force and let it spiral around your physical body, and give thanks.

This short exercise can be practiced frequently. If you use a leaf instead of a flower, sense the fragrance of outdoors and nature for step 8.

As you can see, you are using and exercising both levels of Consciousness in this exercise. It doesn't take long at all to combine these levels. Practice often and always allow time for contemplation after any esoteric exercise. To understand the progress of your Psychic Development, it would be a good idea to keep a journal. Long after you have developed your psychic skills you will appreciate and enjoy looking back at your path of study. This is especially valuable if you become a teacher or counselor, as you will remember from your own references the obstacles and joys of esoteric discovery. In any case, your journal of Psychic Development will become a personal treasure. Be sure to record your early endeavors; this will make it all the more interesting.

When you feel you have achieved the skill to practice the previous exercise properly, then you will be ready for the next exercise. Be sure to make notes on the insights received, especially during the time of contemplation after each study period.

EXERCISE 8: MERGING WITH THE HIGHER SELF

Make your usual pre-meditation arrangements. Dress loosely and remove jewelry, tight belts and shoes, etc. Make sure that you are not going to be disturbed. Lighting a candle will enhance the vibratory atmosphere. Allow yourself a little time to unwind and relax before starting your exercise. Choose a time when you are feeling alert and can appreciate the benefits of this esoteric level. Falling asleep results in disappointment, and you will not derive the benefits of disciplined esoteric study.

1. Come in to the Heart center. Focus all your attention and visualize a bright GOLD center.
   (Wait.)

2. Begin your breathing pattern by inhaling GOLD energy in through the center of the Heart and releasing GOLD out through the Inner Eye. Continue breathing this way and feel the GOLD center of the Heart chakra expanding.
   (Wait.)

3. As the Heart center expands in GOLD, you are also clearing

any blockage or negativity from the Inner Eye area. When the Heart center is full, you will change the breathing pattern. Hold your focus until you are ready.
(Wait.)

4. Now your center is full of GOLD energy. Take four short intakes of breath, followed by one deep slow breath. As you inhale the long slow breath, see a strong GOLD rod lift up from the Heart center to the Inner Eye. As the GOLD rod touches the Inner Eye it is like a magnificent sunburst. Let the rays extend and pulsate from the Inner Eye.
(Wait.)

5. From the center of your GOLD sunburst in the Inner Eye, take in four short breaths followed by one deep slow breath. As you inhale the long slow breath, slowly feel the strong GOLD rod lifting up to the center top of the head to the Crown chakra. As the GOLD rod reaches the Crown chakra, feel once again a magnificent release. The force creates a burst of energy in the Crown chakra. Let the rays stretch out and see the never-ending light pierce the darkness above your head.
(Wait.)

6. Breathing normally, feel the brilliant rays going beyond all impossible vision. Become the center of this spiritual experience. The light is now coming from your body, your fingers and toes. You are suspended in the Universe and you are surrounded by the powerful light you have created. Feel this power—feel the cleansing—feel the urge to release your Conscious level and merge with your Higher Self.
(Wait.)

7. Each normal breath you take increases the light around you. Look directly ahead and you will see the PURPLE light of the Master. Focus on this light as the Master comes nearer.
(Wait.)

8. See yourself reaching out with your hands and touching the PURPLE radiance of the Master.
(Wait.)

9. Your Master turns and asks you to follow. Walking directly into the light, follow the Master to the VIOLET dome ahead. When you arrive at the dome, observe all you see, as this must be recorded later.
(Wait.)

10. You are now standing before the Dome of Wisdom. You will find your Higher Self somewhere within this dome. Your Master now beckons you to follow him into the dome. As you step inside, you feel the warmth of pulsating VIOLET rays. You see many other doors and hallways. Before you is a table. Lying on the table is a scroll. Your Master informs you that the scroll contains the name of your Higher Self. Ask the Master when you may look at the scroll. Listen carefully, for you will be asked to release any remaining negativity. This you will do, as the Master waits.
(Wait.)

11. The Master now tells you to look down at your feet. You see the gray residue of negativity at your feet. You must take this negativity out of the Dome of Wisdom before pursuing your esoteric journey. The Master opens the doors. Take the negativity out of the Dome of Wisdom. It is dark and you are alone. The negativity appears to have grown, yet it engulfs you in a warm familiar way. Call now clearly and loudly for the Angel Oriel. Call "AUUUU—REEEE—EL. AUUUU— REEEE—EL. AUUUU—REEEE—EL."
(Wait.)

12. As the angel Oriel appears, ask that you may receive spiritual help to release the remaining negativity. Listen to what he says.
(Wait.)

13. Make a promise and a vow, saying:

"I make this vow to my Master and the Angel Oriel.
I will pursue my spiritual journey.
I know that negativity is fear.
I cast my fears away.
I can, with this blessing, reach my Higher Self. Amen."

Watch the negativity disappear and disintegrate. When this is complete, the Angel Oriel points to the Dome of Wisdom.
(Wait.)

14. As the doors open, you Master smiles and beckons you to step inside. Behind you, the Angel Oriel extends His holy light and you can feel the power.
(Wait.)

15. Go again to the table and see your scroll. Open it and see the name of your Higher Self.
(Wait.)

16. The Master now calls you by this name and asks you to find your Higher Self. He will wait by the table. Go now and explore your dome. As you explore the dome, call for your Higher Self by name. Each time you hear yourself repeat the name of your Higher Self, you gain more and more strength. The Higher Self is in the center of the Dome of Wisdom. When you see the brilliance of WHITE light pulsating in the center of the dome, kneel and wait.
(Wait.)

17. Now say:
"I come to merge with my Higher Self.
I am here to seek and learn the truth."
Now, from your Heart center, call the name from the scroll and wait for your Higher Self to come before you.
(Wait.)

18. Feel the joy of the spirit before you. Experience the beauty and power of your Higher Self. Look and observe the many unused qualities your Higher Self has brought.
(Wait.)

19. The Higher Self extends open arms. Step forward and merge with your Higher Self. Feel the power gushing into you. Hear the Higher Self call you by the right name. Listen for words of wisdom as you embrace.
(Wait.)

20. As you release the embrace, feel the swift cool vibrations now

rushing around your body. Bow your head and give thanks.
(Wait.)

21. With head still bowed, say farewell to your Master. Rest for awhile as the energies within the dome penetrate every part of your being.
(Wait.)

22. As you stand, the dome doors are wide open. Step out into light and focus on your Inner Eye and down into your Heart chakra. Take in a deep breath and slowly release the energy. You are now stabilized, balanced and ready to change your life.

CHAPTER ELEVEN

THE CENTER OF POWER

You are the Center of Power! Once you discover the power and learn how to increase it through the exercises, you are ready to use the power. The skill with which you use this power will determine the proficiency of your Psychic Development.

A baby has a voice that can be exceptionally loud and demanding. Until the baby learns how to use the voice to speak, we hear baby noises! It isn't difficult to get an idea of what the baby wants—but isn't it good when he can put his needs into words? Likewise, with your newly developed power. Learning how to use it well and efficiently is the next step. A good place to start is with you. Applying this power with skill to enrich your life will not only prove your ability, but also increase it. For as you give, you will receive.

I feel that the serious student needs to allocate a specific period of time to understand the Center of Power. As you learn how to draw on it, you *become* the source. Your power will develop and increase according to how it is used. The power of Spirit is available to all. Looking at life in this way, we see that man is in the center of his own light. As man walks on the karmic path of destiny, he tends to work with his Conscious level and ignore the rest of his strength.

Once you learn how to extract this strength, the karmic obstacles can be understood and overcome. Relationships become easier and our level of tolerance rises as we spiritually develop. Many dilemmas are born of ignorance. The human mind can accept situations where it feels forced to undergo certain conditions. As soon as we realize that we cannot find an answer or logical reason, then we react and trouble begins.

Developing psychic ability helps solve these dilemmas, which are often karmic in nature. A deeper level of sensitivity occurs. Then when the Conscious mind has difficulty accepting a particular circumstance, the esoteric scholar resorts to his intuitive skills and is given insight.

THROUGH SELF

An ancient secret worth learning is that the journey of the esoteric student is "through self." The apparent obstacles that loom before us are clues to the karmic path. The ancient Masters accepted these obstacles as esoteric riddles. Examining the situation, they would probe back to the beginning. Relationships were considered—personal involvements resulting in a spiritual analysis that had to be truthful and objective.

Students of today are capable of the same procedure. The fear of self-analysis is the fear of discovering that you were to blame. This is an example of giving energy to the ego. Knowingly or unknowingly, these ancient practices seem to be avoided because they require being precise and dealing with the resulting analysis.

The mysterious journey "through self" takes you to many secret places. The ultimate achievement is the Center of Power. The esoteric plans seem complex, requiring a great deal of concentration and energy. You may see it this way, as many have. The complexity is seen from a Conscious level and therein lies the (non-existing) problem. Of course it is difficult when you consider all this from the wrong level! The simplicity lies in recognizing that the required energy and ability stem from the Higher Consciousness, which, if known and developed, will rapidly remove all the barriers.

DIRECT ROUTE

As you begin to test and try your intuitive power, avoid any detours. First you go to the source, which is the center of who you are.

From the source, you go directly to your Point of Concentration.

This is not as easy as it sounds, because there are pitfalls. When the Conscious mind becomes aware of the incoming surge of Higher Consciousness, it resists. It immediately takes you back to reality, the reality you know. This is the normal, everyday function of Consciousness. It has the power to present an immediate picture of possibility. At the same time it has a warning device, and renders an alert or alarm whenever you wander off your usual track. This protective energy endeavors to prevent you from experiencing unknown stress whenever you elect to explore new frontiers of thought and action.

It is a kind and familiar energy. The Conscious level is considerate of all your fears and limitations. It is also capable of being controlled by your Higher Consciousness. Your karmic path of destiny can continue as a mysterious journey, or be enlightened through the wisdom of your Higher Self. It may seem strange that the Conscious level, which deals with everyday emotions, actions and situations, is actually a misconceived focus. From the Conscious level we expect to see everything clearly. Yet we deceive ourselves. What appears to be clear and concise is actually unreal. In the disguise of clarity, the Conscious level prevents us from seeing and being in touch with the reality of our karma.

The Conscious mind is reluctant to allow the light of the Higher Consciousness to come through. Without this light or Higher contact, you are destined to deal with each day as it comes. But if you use the Higher Consciousness, you will have a much wider vision of your original intent and purpose.

Only by operating directly from the center of who you are will you see the wide vista of possibility. Narrowing yourself to the comfortable and protective level of everyday Consciousness prohibits you from seeing the complete picture.

And it isn't a question of functioning only on one level or another. Whenn you recognize the center of who you are, you have access to other probabilities. You become exposed to your own inner strength and you are able to develop a new competency in exercising choice. It is not a case of all or nothing. You can use the level of Consciousness that suits the particular situation.

As you start your day, the Conscious level will try its best to give you an idea of what you may expect. If the ideas submitted have sufficient emotional content, then you are confronted with the need to operate on the Conscious level and on the Emotional level as well. So you become burdened with apprehension even before the day starts. Knowing that "thoughts are living things," we can see that even before you finish your bowl of cereal you have already started your day. How many times have you gone to work full of fear and apprehension? Instead of doing new things and using your energies on new situations, you allow the Conscious mind to limit your expression. The built-in sense of caution becomes a resisting force that deliberately prevents you from venturing into new and exciting possibilities.

The alternative is quite easy. Come to the Center of Power. This is your own center. Making decisions from this point will allow you to use the correct level of Consciousness. Each level will then operate according to the needs established by your Higher Self in your Center of Power. Your personal access is not difficult. In fact, you can start using it immediately. Any time you feel a restriction in thought, word or deed, come into your own Center of Power. It is here you will discover your alternate choices. Your Center of Power contains strength and the vision to see all future potential.

EXERCISE 9: COMING INTO YOUR CENTER

This exercise helps you come directly to your center. Soon it will be an easy and natural thing to do. You will be able to come into your center and focus without any distraction. This exercise can be used as an esoteric tool. Whenever you feel limited, use this exercise to free yourself from restricting energies.

Each time you change from one important life cycle to another, you will recognize the nature and content of the incoming cycle. (It may be a Personal Life Cycle; see *Connolly Book of Numbers*, vols. 1 and 2 or, an important change of Cyclotone; see *Karma Without Stress*.)

Any time you feel the impact of change, go to the center of your own power. Only from this esoteric level can you determine if the change is part of your karmic destiny. To really obtain the full benefit of this exercise, make a point of *not* making major decisions until you have experienced the wisdom found in your Center of Power.

Each time you enter your Center of Power you will be given wisdom and insight regarding a relationship. Before the meditation, choose someone with whom you feel you have karmic ties. Write the name of this person on a piece of WHITE paper. Fold it in half twice, and place it by the WHITE candle.

Prepare for your meditation exercise in the usual way. Dress loosely and remove any distracting jewelry. Make sure that you won't be disturbed. Lighting a candle is always conducive to meditation. I recommend you use a WHITE candle for this exercise.

1. Begin by concentrating on the Crown chakra, located at the center top of the head. Bring all your energy up to this point and visualize a WHITE disc of light.
    (Wait.)

2. As the light begins to solidify, breathe in slowly and easily from your feet up to the WHITE disc of light at the top of your head. Hold your breath for a count of three. Release the breath down through your body and visualize it flowing out from your feet.
    (Wait.)

3. Each time you inhale your WHITE breath, feel yourself merging with the light of the Crown chakra. As the breath goes down the body and out through the feet, know that all negativity is now being released. Continue to breathe this way.
    (Wait.)

4. Now feel a beautiful energy surrounding you. Light is coming from your Crown chakra. As the vibrant energy coils around your body in a gentle motion, feel all your power concentrated in the WHITE light of the Crown chakra.
    (Wait.)

5. Relax as you feel the protective WHITE energies spinning around your body.
    (Wait.)

6. The Crown chakra is brilliant at the top of your head. Your body is wrapped in glowing WHITE energies. Bring your attention to the Inner Eye and, as you look before you, there is

a beautiful Cobalt BLUE energy. As the energy builds in strength, you can feel the intense BLUE vibrations coming toward you. Gradually you feel yourself being gently pushed back. It is a wonderful and healing experience.
(Wait.)

7. The Cobalt BLUE now touches every part of your body. You are moving back; you are being taken to your Center of Power.
(Wait.)

8. Behind you is a WHITE throne. You can feel the power of the throne as you come closer. As you move back, your Master appears in the Cobalt BLUE energy before you.
(Wait.)

9. Your Master now takes your hand. You turn around and see your Center of Power. Sit on the throne and feel the impact of your inner strength.
(Wait.)

10. As you sit on your throne, see everything now change into pure WHITE light. See how your vibratory force reaches far out beyond you. Ask your Master to show you any present difficulties or dilemmas. They will be crystal-clear, and you now have the inner power to analyze and understand them. If you have questions, ask your Master. He is always with you and always ready to give the support and wisdom of the Master Level. Spend this time well.
(Wait.)

11. You are now ready to use your new vision. From the Center of Power you are going to see a karmic re-play of any previous relationship you had with the person whose name is written on the WHITE paper. What you will see is important and relevant to the nature and circumstance of your present relationship.
(Wait.)

12. Your Master now stands before you and gives you words of wisdom. Listen carefully.
(Wait.)

13. Remain seated on your throne in your Center of Power. Breathe in WHITE light and breathe out WHITE light. (Wait.)

14. Stand now and step forward into the Cobalt BLUE energy. Feel yourself swiftly moving forward and bring the clarity of your new Consciousness through the healing BLUE energies. (Wait.)

15. Everything becomes still, soul-still around you. The WHITE light is now cleansing every aspect of your aura. Stand still and feel the colors in your aura being balanced to their true color level. Feel your aura stretching out to every part of your life. (Wait.)

16. Make your affirmation slowly and sincerely:
    "I have found my Center of Power.
    I am full of abundance and energy.
    I will use the wisdom I have learned.
    I know the source of my true spirituality. Amen."

Take time and contemplate all the wisdom that has been given. Make notes in your journal, and be determined to control your life from your Center of Power.

CHAPTER TWELVE

THE AURA

The esoteric division and separation of energies surrounding the physical body is quite complex. When we speak of the "aura" in esoteric terms, it is usually in reference to the psychic energy field surrounding both animate and inanimate bodies.

A normal healthy aura can extend six-to-seven feet beyond the physical body. The colors vary, representing vibratory energies that originate as a result of your inner equilibrium. Your physical and mental balance is reflected through your aura. You are not born with a green aura or a blue aura! Your aura is a reflection of what is happening internally on many different levels, and it is interpreted accordingly.

Think of your aura as a reflection of how you think and feel. A well-balanced aura is radiant and can extend far beyond the normal six-to-seven feet. The aura also acts as an antenna. Auras can touch and merge without physical contact! Walking in a grocery store, from one office to another, at work or play—auras are exposed to the energies of other auras.

This could account for the way we feel with different people. Being with someone you love is comfortable. If the relationship is intense you can also feel vulnerable. Sometimes you meet someone and you feel awful, or dreadfully uncomfortable. This can happen standing in line at the theater or sitting in the library reading a book. Whenever you feel this way you will find that, if you move away, your inner equilibrium will feel balanced again.

Exposure to unbalanced auras can affect you in many ways. If your own inner balance is good then you will quickly recover your equilibrium. During my years of research I have also discovered that a person can be governed by the influence of dominant aura rays from another person. If you are feeling low or depressed, you are more apt to absorb the vibratory flow of someone else's aura—good, bad or indifferent. I have also found that we can adapt quite easily to the vibratory force of others.

THE BABY AND THE AURA

Before a baby is born, its aura is established but it is not necessarily active. Within the force field of the mother's aura, the baby first learns to blend its own identity with that of the mother. This, of course, is the reason mothers always seem to know exactly what their children are up to! Gradually, as the child grows and develops his own strength, he subconsciously chooses to cut himself off from his mother's vibratory influence. This cutting-off has nothing to do with a person's love for their mother. It is the need to establish one's own force field. Where there is an extraordinary love and/or karmic connection, there is never a complete severance between child and mother.

In experimental regressive therapy, there are situations where a person has retained the memory of happenings in the home and family prior to physical birth. This unusual type of situation has occurred when the mother underwent undue stress during pregnancy. It is also not uncommon for a baby to retain a definite memory pattern of events prior to birth, yet have no memory of the physical birth process itself.

As the baby grows in the womb, so does its aura. The baby can be susceptible to outside influences, especially in the latter stages before birth. After the baby is born, there is an undetermined period of time when it is adjusting to its new physical environment and to the balance and projection of its aura field.

Both parents often sense the connecting energies of the child. Any previous karmic relationship they may have had with the baby becomes an integral part of the family structure. There is a knowing and a belonging, regardless of behavior or family similarity—an extra-special tie. This is translated as love and becomes part of the relationship. The aura is the first way we begin to know each other. We either like what we feel, or we don't. Children use this ability quite early. They are quick to let you know if they like a person or like being in a particular place. Parents should watch how the child reacts and not be too quick to reprimand. After all, the child is responding to a natural inclination. (Obviously, I am not referring to times when a child is being difficult or just plain naughty.)

A baby shows its displeasure, even with its eyes closed, if it feels any kind of discomfort. Until the aura has found its true balance, a baby will usually allow any loving person to hold it. After a few weeks it becomes more discerning. When a baby is transferred lovingly into someone's waiting arms, the child will react strongly if it feels a disturbance within its aura.

THE AURA IMAGE

The aura reflects the condition of all levels of Consciousness. A person with natural clairvoyant vision can easily assess the continuous and changing vibratory patterns. A person with normal vision can look and describe what he sees. For example, if a teacher and student both observed a scientific test at the same time, they would see the same thing. If we then asked both the teacher and the student what had actually happened, the student would explain it to the best of his ability. The teacher, who had prior knowledge of the project, would explain exactly what had happened. Two clairvoyants, one with natural knowledge, the other a student, would present an analogous situation. Too often, it is taken for granted that because a person has a natural psychic ability, they automatically are able to translate a precise and correct interpretation of what they see. When I was young, I saw the continuous movement of changing color bands around certain people, and I interpreted what I saw. Only after study and learning did I really understand what I saw.

This is why we can have so many variations and translations of the color strata formed by the aura. There would be an exception, of course, if a person were clairaudient as well as clairvoyant. Such a person could see clairvoyantly and communicate clairaudiently. In a case like this, the medium would be receiving an ongoing commentary regarding his clairvoyant vision. So as we can see there are many intriguing forms of natural psychic ability. Maybe you have had a glimpse of an aura. This can be quite exciting. The following exercise shows how to develop your ability to see auras. This exercise is excellent for group study, as students can participate with each other. Working with different partners will allow you to tune into the varied energy levels.

Initially, the aura may be seen as gray or white mist around the head. With continued practice, the aura can eventually be seen in full color.

> Color is vibration.
> Vibration is sound.
> Sound is tone.
> Tone is color.

EXERCISE TEN: SEEING THE AURA

This exercise requires two students, working with each other. Loose clothing is quite important in this exercise. Remove all distracting jewelry and have comfortable seating positions. Partner A is the student who is observing the aura. Partner B is the student who is relaxing and allowing Partner A to observe his aura.

In their early stages of Psychic Development, both partners should spend a short time relaxing. During this time every effort should be made by both people to release all negativity.

PARTNER B:

1. Be comfortable and free of tension.

2. Sit in front of a clear wall, one with no pictures or mirrors that might cause distraction for Partner A.

3. Throughout the exercise, eyes must be closed.

4. Visualize WHITE Light around the head, and relax.

5. Remain this way until the exercise is finished.

PARTNER A:

1. Breathe in WHITE Light through the Crown chakra (center top of head). Release the outgoing breath through the Inner Eye (top of the nose, center of eyebrows).

2. As you release the breath, visualize the energy going directly to the Inner Eye of Partner B.

3. Relax as much as possible and continue to breathe in a gentle easy rhythm.

4. Soon you will see an energy forming around the head of Partner B.

5. THIS IS THE CRUCIAL PART OF THE EXERCISE! Your natural inclination will be to shift your gaze from your partner's Inner Eye and look at the forming aura energy. RESIST THIS TEMPTATION. If you move from your Point of Concentration, you will lose the esoteric vision.

6. Allow the energy to form, keeping your focus on the Inner Eye of Partner B.

7. When you begin to see the energy of the aura, stay relaxed and start to breathe normally.

8. When your vision fades and *before* you begin to talk to your partner, write down exactly what you saw and how it happened.

9. It is possible that you might receive some psychic impression. Be sure to write clearly whatever you receive.

10. When you have recorded the exercise, then you can ask your partner to open his eyes.

Here are some additional tips for success with this exercise:

1. Both partners should be prepared to respect each other's part in this exercise.

2. As long as you maintain silence you will hold the vibratory level.

3. Making notes before you speak will enable you to have a clear and concise journal.

4. Be alert for any psychic impression that you experience during the exercise.

5. Before you exchange your partner positions take a small break so that each of you are ready to take a different part in the exercise.

The teacher and the students may find it most interesting to break away from the original partner and share the exercise with another class member. This will enable the student to see that all auras are not the same shape, size or color.

Some students work better with other students, depending on the esoteric compatibility. First, the student should learn to see the aura using the exercise procedures. Once this is accomplished he will be able to use his ability easily in a non-formal way—sitting in a restaurant, relaxing at home or in any other ordinary situation.

Working with a friend and sharing your experiences can help considerably with your early Psychic Development. Seeing an aura can often trigger other intuitive senses. This is why I stress the importance of keeping a journal.

Maybe you don't belong to a Development group or don't have a friend to work with. If this is the case, you can still develop your ability to see auras. Using the above relaxation procedure, sit in a comfortable armchair or on a couch with a soft support for the arm.

1. Begin by placing your left arm in a comfortable position so you can easily look at your hand.

2. Breathe in through your Crown chakra, and breathe out through the Inner Eye. Visualize the outgoing breath entering the entire center of the palm.

3. Keep your vision focused on the center of the hand. When you see the aura energy extending from the fingers, keep your original focus in the center and begin to breathe normally.

4. After the energies subside, record your progress and any psychic impressions you might have received.

PSYCHOMETRY

Psychometry is a simple psychic procedure, allowing one's natural intuitive power to touch the vibratory force that surrounds all things. Every object has an energy surrounding it, and this energy becomes personalized by its owner. The energy contains sufficient power to reveal activities, thoughts and images to someone who knows the skill of psychometry.

The longer a person has had the object, the easier it is to practice the art of psychometry. Any kind of object will do. The object should be personal, something that a person frequently uses or wears. A ring, watch or bracelet that has been worn for quite some time will provide much better information than an article that is seldom used.

To practice psychometry, step aside from your normal thought process, and permit your Higher Self to relate information. These are the skills of the psychometrist. The subtle flow of sensitivity from the Higher Self impregnates your Conscious level in many different ways. But when we are in "full control," we are simply not open to the signals continually coming from the Higher Self. Making a deliberate effort to be receptive is in itself the skill of psychometry.

The questions people usually ask about psychometry are: How does it all work? Can I do it? What do I have to do?

HOW DOES PSYCHOMETRY WORK?

No one really knows! It does not appear to be related to the accepted five senses. Dr. C. G. Jung wrote about the Collective Unconscious. He was referring to a body of knowledge separated, set aside, from the normal levels of Consciousness. He believed that all human beings have a connecting link to this source; that, under certain conditions, man is able to extract from this Universal body of information.

The information is then transferred to the normal level of Consciousness, revealing hitherto-unknown data.

The Collective Unconscious is recognized in many ways. It is the source of unseen energy that contains all wisdom and knowledge. It is the God Force, the Universal Force, the divine level of Consciousness that holds all things. Man can and does avail himself of this pure energy. It is said that everything man is and does is recorded on this level. But it is not limited just to man's activities, like the akashic records. It goes far beyond that concept.

This divine force permeates every living thing within and without the world as we know it. It is the soul of existence, the soul of all things. It contains the beginning, and all things now and future. It is complete and indestructible, representing the holiest of holies and the true source of all spirituality. It is the ultimate power and majesty of all the heavens.

Everyone and everything has its own individual place of spirituality. Since time began, man has searched for this Missing Link. Individual spirituality cannot be severed from its very source. We have the Missing Link to this divine source. The way we express our individual spirituality determines the measure or flow available to us.

How does it all work? Very simply. Learn how to release the natural defense system of the Conscious level. Be open to all the divine elements. Freely accept the natural flow of Universal Energy and, in translating, neither add nor subtract from the powerful input of truth. Refuse to analyze or compromise the intelligence being transmitted. Look beyond your personal purpose and be aware of the responsibility incurred when you relate information you receive. That is how it works.

CAN I PRACTICE PSYCHOMETRY?

You do it all the time—you really do! The Universal Force constantly replenishes your life energy. When the mind feels the urge or motivation to explore beyond its normal limitations, it also accepts the responsibility of analysis. From that point on it becomes more alert and discriminating. There is a constant sorting of data which necessitates the need to determine the source of information received.

Once the Conscious level realizes it cannot account for certain pieces of information, it is then obliged to investigate the source. The first step is usually the amazement of recognizing that this ability has always existed, previously thought of as "intuition," perhaps, or just unknown. In fact, intuition is nothing more than a tool to gain insight or to extend the normal thinking process. It is from this point that any form of Psychic Development takes place.

The Universal flow of divine energy is accessible to all human beings. You may elect to use a particular method of Divination to express your own personal flow. But the source of energy is always identical. How it is *used* is very personal. It is the same energy we call "love" and "compassion." It is truth, and healing, and the need to help others through friendship, counseling or Divination. How you use the Universal Force is your personal choice and expression. This is the ultimate responsibility of spirituality.

Our question is, "Can I do it?" The answer is yes. Which way you choose becomes a matter of personal choice determined by your individual spiritual structure. *Gnothi Seauton*—"Know Thyself" is the starting point. Knowing what is good and what is right for you is the spiritual ingredient. From this vantage point, you can soar into the Universal spheres of knowledge and receive abundant wisdom. It all begins with a willingness to develop your awareness. Foster your inner desire to explore your spiritual potential. Be open to the inner guidance you receive.

You must contribute to your own development. You just can't expect it to happen all on its own. Nurture the need to know and understand. These simple requirements will provide you with a new and exciting spiritual outlook.

WHAT DO I HAVE TO DO?

Using the skill of psychometry is being aware of the vibratory force that surrounds all things. An article that is used, worn or carried on a regular basis is the ideal starting point. Resist the limitations of the Conscious level. Hold the item in question and allow the Conscious mind to accept what you are doing. Ignore the inner doubts and, as you hold the object, wait until you receive information. The information can reveal itself in many ways. A psychometrist may hear, see or feel the nature of the energy surrounding the article.

Keep in mind that the initial impressions are unrelated to you. What you hear, see or feel is not normally what you would hear, see or feel. You are tuning into another energy stream. Because it is unfamiliar to your own sensitive system, you could very well dismiss the information that is trying to decode itself through your esoteric connection. Whichever way your Conscious mind becomes impregnated with the unfamiliar information, you should release it exactly as you receive it.

"I can hear . . . ."
"I see . . . ."
"I feel . . . ."

Avoid using words that you don't hear, see or feel. Your skill will develop rapidly if you recognize that you are only an instrument. Through your capacity and sensitivity you can touch the Universal source. Being a psychometrist does not restrict you to any particular method of sensitivity. When holding an object, you will discover that some aspect of your being is ultra-sensitive—part of you is speaking and relating information, while the Conscious level may be questioning your competence to do so. Avoid this inner conflict and, when practicing psychometry, be open to receive.

FIRST SKILLS OF THE PSYCHOMETRIST

In the following simple procedures lie the skill of psychometry. Before you actually start testing your ability, try the following preliminary exercises. The Power of Concentration is important. Learn how to focus above the normal Conscious level. Once your mind shifts and submits to the input of the Higher Consciousness, psychometry is comparatively easy.

Consider these preliminary procedures as mental "push-ups." The more you exercise, the quicker you will attain your goal. To begin, learn to control your focus on everyday objects. During ordinary mundane chores, we usually allow the mind total freedom—depending, of course, on the kind of work we are doing. In a situation where you feel free in allowing the mind to wander, use that time to exercise your concentration power.

EXERCISE 11: HOW TO FOCUS

The mind is what the brain does. So when you endeavor to change your level of Consciousness, it is necessary to register this information with the brain cells. Otherwise, the mind has a tendency to flit here and there. If you think of the brain as a computer, and the mind as the program disk, you can see that the first thing to do is to turn the computer on. The next step is to use the computer controls to prepare for the program you wish to use.

Learning to focus is pretty much the same procedure. Begin by bringing all your attention to one object. This is not only entertaining, it is educational. Just imagine yourself turning on your "brain computer" and directing all your concentration to a small item. Take a pen, for example. If you casually look at a pen, very quickly your mind will absorb all that it sees and advise you that it is a pen. Exercising your individual power, you say, "That is not enough; tell me more about the pen."

Examining the Object

The pen:

1. What is the length of the pen?
2. What is the circumference of the pen?
3. What color is the case?
4. What color is the ink?
5. What type of a pen is it?
6. Who manufactured it?
7. Does it have a separate top?
8. Is it automatic?
9. Is it a fountain pen?

10. How many colors are on the pen?

11. What is it made of?

12. Is it an inexpensive pen?

13. Is it expensive?

14. Who does it belong to?

15. Where did you get it?

16. How long have you had it?

17. Do you use it often?

18. Do you like to write with it?

19. When did you last use it?

20. Why?

Just a simple list of twenty questions—and there could be more. Simply writing that list and looking at my pen caused my memory cells to function. I was provided with information I had previously stored. Some of the information was interesting—like how I got the pen. Some was mundane and I felt my mind wanting to stretch out to other areas.

Focus, then, requires self-control. Choose any object and try this exercise. Each time your mind feels inclined to go on, bring it back firmly, then replace your focus. The more you practice this exercise, the easier it becomes. It really is wonderful for reviving old forgotten memories that you have stored at some other time. Try to isolate your object so you will not shift your focus. It is better to place the object before you, rather than in your hand. This way, you won't be tempted to let your attention go to rings or watches, or anything that will distract attention. If you keep your eyes on the item, this helps. Don't look around the room or at other things. With regular practice you will soon develop the ability to examine, probe and ask yourself many questions about the object.

Transferring Your Focus

Once you develop a proficiency in concentration and focus, you will be ready to apply this skill to objects belonging to others. When you do this, remember that psychometry is the skill of interpreting exactly what you feel or receive without justifying it.

For example, a drummer may enjoy the rhythm and sound of the drums. Another person could have an entirely different reaction to the same sound. This is why it's important that the psychometrist reveal exactly what is received, rather than giving an interpretation. If you were to tell the drummer you sense loud noise and the inability to think, the drummer may think you are speaking of Beethoven's Fifth Symphony! Likewise with color. Never refer to a color as "unattractive"—describe it as you see or feel it. Some years ago in a beginning class I had two students working with each other. One student expressed how happy she felt, but that she could not understand "the terrible green dress," which was obviously an important part of her psychometry reading. Eventually the second student responded and told her it was the dress she had worn for her second marriage. She liked that shade of green!

Suggesting ideas to correspond with what you are feeling defeats the whole purpose of psychometry. Let the holder of the article find his own clues, as you relate exactly what you receive. If you dwell on the article long enough you will pick up scattered pieces of information. The owner of the object will soon fit all these pieces together and admire your skill as a psychometrist.

Here is a list of do's and don't's for the psychometrist—a basic list of instructions. You will soon develop your own style and expression. If you require a little time to absorb the surrounding energies before speaking, then it's wise to explain that to the owner of the article. Or, you may discover that you have an aptitude for tuning into exact data, yet you lose it if you are asked questions. If this is so, tell the owner before you start.

Do's and Don't's

DO:	DON'T:
Take your time to experience.	Feel hurried.
Follow the right procedure.	Take shortcuts.
Ask for older articles.	Work with new items.

Tell the owner how you work.	Work any other way.
Say exactly what you receive.	Exaggerate.
Convey small details.	Discard anything.
Get another item if needed.	Continue if blank.
Be relaxed and focused.	Work if noisy.
Say, "I hear," "I see," "I feel."	Try to interpret.
Stop when you feel tired.	Do just one more!

An interesting and wonderful way to try the Do's and Don't's is to choose an old family object. You may really enjoy working with old familiar objects and surprisingly pick up information you didn't know. It can be rewarding and fun to check what you receive with family members.

Psychometry Objects

Here is an ideal list of objects to use for psychometry:

Pen	Watch	Book	Comb
Letter	Necklace	Old coin	Mirror
Key	Ring	Old document	Scarf
Key-ring	Bracelet	Photograph	Old toy

I'm sure you can and will add to this list. Remember, the older the item, the easier it is for you to pick up the vibratory force. Depending on your mediumistic tendencies, you may receive quite a lot of information about the original owner.

White Light

Before and after this exercise (or any spiritual exercise or practice), it is good to protect yourself with pure White Light. This clears all negativity and creates the correct spiritual atmosphere.

1. Visualize a ball of White Light beneath the feet.

2. Visualize breathing IN from this ball of White Light.

3. As you INHALE White breath, bring it up from beneath your feet to the highest point possible above your head.

4. Release and exhale the breath as White Light, and let it fall down through the body and beneath the feet, forming a White Pyramid of Light from above the head to below the feet. Quietly say, "Amen."

EXERCISE 12: PRACTICING PSYCHOMETRY

This is a very simple but effective procedure. Ask for the kind of object you prefer to work with. Step away from the owner and follow these instructions:

1. Visualize a thin WHITE line of energy going from the Inner Eye (top of the nose between the eybrows) down to the Emotional level (located just above the natural waistline, directly under the rib cage).

2. Visualize the thin WHITE energy moving rapidly between these two points; at the same time, hold the object in your right hand, placing it directly on the Emotional level.

3. Allow the WHITE line of energy to move rapidly between the two centers, until you feel it stabilize and become a strong, firm rod of WHITE energy.

4. You are now ready to receive the impact of energy surrounding the object.

5. Still holding the article in your right hand against the Emotional level, concentrate now on the object, and relate what you receive. Avoid trying to please or reason with the information. Just relax and convey exactly what you see, hear and feel. These are the initial skills of the psychometrist.

6. Once the information is flowing in, let your hands come slightly forward and hold the item between both hands.

7. If you feel a drop or lack of energy bring the right hand back to the Emotional level holding the object. Establish again a firm rod of WHITE energy until it stabilizes.

CHAPTER THIRTEEN

AUTOMATISM

Automatism is a term used in parapsychology that refers to paranormal activities done without Conscious awareness. This area of parapsychology is quite complex. There are psychic functions that are interrelated, and others that are simply offshoots of another function. Essentially each individual method comes from the same ancient root of esoteric practice. These old methods of psychic expression have become more and more sophisticated through the ages.

Spiritual activities preceded by the word "automatic" are considered specialized psychic skills, such as:

Automatic Writing   Automatic Drawing
Automatic Painting   Automatic Speaking

MOTOR AUTOMATISM

Some forms of automatism occur without apparent control or Conscious intent. This category is generally known as *motor automatism*. Motor automatism occurs when a person is able to retain a normal level of Consciousness yet an energy manifests itself through the physical body. It is similar to when a person has a nervous twitch in the eye, for example. It happens and the Conscious mind cannot physically control it. Some examples of motor automatism are using a pendulum; sleepwalking; moving a glass tumbler; tilting a table.

There are distinct differences of approach and Consciousness when dealing with automatism and motor automatism. These are personal automatism and group automatism.

Group study can be helpful in that you can readily discover in a class whether you have a natural aptitude.

Automatism is usually conducted in a trancelike state, and the medium is on a different level of Consciousness. Some claim that during the process they are unaware, and they believe that the spirit of someone who has passed over is responsible. Another theory is that some people unknowingly can shift their level of Consciousness and perform, create or produce skills, information and talent that are not considered a normal part of their personality. This would indicate that there is a part of the personality that can produce these things that appear unrelated and require a point of focus other than what is usually used.

IDENTIFYING THE SOURCE

Either way, it would appear that ordinary people have produced some outstanding works of poetry, writing, art and speaking. The dividing line is often difficult to decipher. Several distinct sources are given credit for automatism:

1. The spirit of someone deceased, transmitting its own knowledge, and communicating through a medium who is in a trancelike situation and unaware of the information being received.

2. The same as above, except that the medium has a partial realization of what is taking place. The medium remains fully aware, yet contributes energy expression from a source other than himself—an input of power attributed to a spiritual identity.

3. A shifting of Consciousness that causes access to brain cells not normally used. A definite change occurs that seemingly enables the medium to provide information or demonstrate skills not considered part of his normal personality. It is thought that gifts and talents used

in a previous life are accessible and located in the brain; and that, under certain conditions, a person is able to avail himself of these past abilities.

4. An undefined ability to be physically receptive to an outside source of energy.

THE CORRECT APPROACH

All psychic communication should be controlled and understood by the participant. There are teachers and schools of learning that help identify and establish the esoteric source of information, and provide the training required. Attempting to induce a trance situation is not advisable without a previous understanding or correct instruction by a professional teacher.

All these practices should be taken seriously. Your state of mind and approach will influence the energy, and determine the nature of information you receive. As with any other study procedure, a serious approach provides the best results.

Keep a journal of your progress and allow a limited amount of time for each study period. Register exactly what you receive and make a note of any questions you ask. Avoid long tiring study periods. If you receive dissatisfactory information or just sheer nonsense, stop what you are doing and begin again at another time. These basic rules will bring you the best results.

AUTOMATIC WRITING

Automatic Writing takes patience and common sense. In the beginning, the hand may be slow to move. It will then possibly progress to an undetermined scribble. From then on, there should be a steady development of writing. The actual handwriting could be any of the following:

1. Your own!
2. A completely different style of handwriting.

3. Multiple styles of handwriting.

However, while the method of communication is "handwriting," the type of handwriting is not the issue. It is the content that has to be considered. If, for example, you feel you are receiving a lot of gibberish, then it doesn't matter how good the actual handwriting may be. Sometimes automatic writing contains pieces of information that are quite spiritual or philosophical. If such writing is genuinely unfamiliar to you in style and content, then it is clearly from a source outside yourself. But you might produce poetic extractions that are really from deeper parts of your own mind. When this happens, a part of you knows it is happening! Discontinue, and begin again.

THE METHOD OF COMMUNICATION

Automatic Writing can be a method of receiving general information from various esoteric levels. Personal guidance and pertinent information relating to your life can be received. Or, you may receive information for others. Often such communication is almost instructional. When writing like this is received and no identity of the source is given, then you should ask who or where the information is coming from. After all, if you can receive two or three paragraphs of information then there should be no difficulty in asking the source for its name.

Another interesting method of communication is like a question-and-answer process. This type of contact is usually developed after the student has accomplished the initial procedures and feels quite comfortable with what they are doing. It usually begins by the source identifying itself. Then you may be asked if you have any questions, or you may be given advice and then invited to ask questions.

You should have strong personal feelings about the input or advice received from another Conscious level. It is important that you know who you are communicating with. Treat yourself with respect and do not be open or available to just "anything." If someone telephoned and didn't give you a name, you wouldn't be likely to sit there and gullibly take so-called advice. Your Conscious level must have the assurance that you are pursuing a serious venture, otherwise you will not be satisfied with the results.

EXERCISE 13: PRACTICING AUTOMATIC WRITING

Sit in a comfortable position. Have ready a smooth-flowing pen that is easy to hold, and a stack of writing paper. Lighting a candle helps to create a good spiritual atmosphere. Allocate a period of time and when your time is finished, complete your study. Make sure that you will not be disturbed. Relax and begin.

1. Hold the pen fairly loosely—just enough to know that you are holding a pen. Remember, you are only supporting the pen, you will not be doing the actual writing.

2. This next point may seem strange but it is important: Allow your mind to wander where it may! Think of what you have done at work today or of a family member, or a particular relationship. Just *don't* think about your hand, the pen or any writing. When the pen begins to write deliberately, steer your thoughts away. Simply let it happen and put your thoughts elsewhere. A good outside focus is reading a book!

3. When you are prepared and have the pen in your hand, create your WHITE Light.

4. You are now ready to receive. You may have to wait a considerable amount of time at first. In any event, when the amount of time you allocated is over, stop the session.

5. It is quite common to first receive squiggles and swirls. Hopefully, this soon progresses into writing. If an energy is going to use your physical hand to write, then at least we should allow a little time for the adjustment.

6. Once you receive a piece of writing and the pen stops, it would be a good idea to ask the energy to identify itself. For some reason, the expectation of results from automatic writing vary from one extreme to the other. In some cases, people have received outstanding evidence of identity and relevant information. On the other hand, you may find nonsensical or childish messages. This is where you make a firm decision. You can choose to continue, or relax for a few moments and then restart, asking for a change of energy.

7. Keep your papers for your personal record. Date your sessions and enjoy your serious approach, as with all esoteric procedures.

Always be persistent in your inquiries, if the writing informs you that you are being advised by a deceased relative, a well-known historical character or any other source. Obtain as much information as possible and do a little research to confirm it.

CHAPTER FOURTEEN

DOWSING

For centuries various forms of a pendulum have been used for Divination. Dowsing is a similar procedure as they both fall into the category of motor automatism.

The dowsing instrument is a divining rod. Usually the serious dowser works with a Y-shaped stick. The ancients used hazel sticks but the modern-day dowser selects and uses a tool of his own choosing. The gifted dowser may not work with a divining rod at all—just by using his outstretched fingers, he can locate the presence of water. The practice of dowsing goes back to the Middle Ages and is practiced now especially in primitive regions. The work of the dowser was important for discovering freshwater springs. A divining rod is also referred to as a magic rod, or Jacob's Rod.

Dowsing is not limited to finding water. Underground metals and lost objects also can be located. A good dowser can even extend his skill to "missing persons." Dowsing is considered a remarkable talent and many reputable people have practiced it.

Each dowser has his own particular technique, which has developed through sheer experience. Generally speaking, a dowser will spend a considerable amount of time walking fastidiously in a selected area. Using his dowsing instrument, he surveys the ground until the divining rod reacts involuntarily, thus indicating the desired location.

Dowsers often specialize. For example, some dowsers can locate water and also determine the depth of the water. Others may specialize in metals and missing objects. Dowsers seemingly possess a unique natural skill. Families have taken pride in passing this ability from generation to generation. The origins of dowsing were born from necessity! People had to have water and this provided the impetus for man to resort to ancient natural skills. Imagine—a total reliance on self that forced an inherent ability to surface!

Perhaps you would like to discover your own dowsing talent. You could start in the backyard, or maybe with a walk in the countryside. Or, use a beach if you live near one, or find a wonderful forest—someplace where you feel private and free to experiment.

The first thing you need to acquire is your own personal divining rod. You may want to experiment with the ancient method of using hazel. The fact is, if you have a strong natural tendency toward dowsing, it really doesn't matter what type of divining rod you use initially. Later, when you have refined your technique, you can enjoy refining your tools. There are several books that will help you determine different shapes, sizes and materials for particular types of dowsing activities.

But in the beginning, select from the following kinds of rods: a natural twig with a Y-shaped end or, a metal rod made from wire, with a Y-shaped end.

The outdoors is more conducive to dowsing than the confines of indoors. Remember, you are exploring the undefined ability to be physically receptive to energies other than your own. Exposure to the outdoors is spiritually invigorating and enhances your own personal energy structure. The next step is to decide what you would like to find with your divining rod. You could choose one of the following: shell, coin, glass, key, flower or water.

Once you decide what it is you wish to find, then you will prepare an Edict. The content of the Edict will be transmitted, along with your desire, to the Higher Consciousness. From this level, the Higher Self will direct the energy required, causing your physical body to become acutely alert when you conduct your search.

For the preparatory exercise, you will need:

White writing paper.

A pen.

Your choice of one of the above six kinds of objects.

A small container, suitable to put the object in.

Your first divining rod, with Y-shaped end.

A notebook to record all details.

A white candle, to enhance your concentration.

EXERCISE 14: PREPARATION FOR DOWSING

1. Select one of these six kinds of objects:
   Shell   Coin   Glass   Key   Flower   Water

2. Write boldly on the top of your paper the name of the object you have chosen. For the purpose of this exercise, we will select a container of water.

3. On a table, have your selected object, your journal, divining rod, writing paper and pen.

4. Light the WHITE candle to increase your concentration and put yourself in WHITE Light.

5. Holding your chosen object and looking at the flame of the candle with your Inner Eye, say:

"I ask that the power of true Divination be increased around me so that I may be aware of the Universal Force. Within the purity of this White candle and the White Light around me, I ask that my intention and purpose be blessed."

Now take the divining rod in your left hand and the container in your right. Holding them near the purity of the flame, say:

"I ask for peace, tranquillity, balance and harmony. I ask that the pure energies of the Universal Force impregnate my humble tool of Divination. I ask for peace, tranquillity, balance and harmony. I ask that I may be guided through purity and light to use this power to find the elements of my token."

With your left hand, touch the object in your right hand. Looking at the flame of the candle with your Inner Eye say:

"It is my promise to the divine power that I have pure intent, and I will diligently keep this promise."

Quietly put down the divining rod to your left, followed by the object to your right. Write the date on your paper and this Edict:

"I KNOW THE UNIVERSAL POWER IS AVAILABLE TO ME. WITH THIS POWER I WILL USE MY TOOL OF DIVINATION TO FIND . . . " (Write what you will be searching for and then sign your name to personalize your Edict.)

DOWSING ENERGY

The prayer in the preparation exercise above should be used each day prior to your dowsing expedition. Building strength and endowing your Edict with your own Conscious energy will make your dowsing more effective. Keep the Edict with you in your handbag or wallet. Each time you see it, your Higher Self will be reminded of your Conscious intent to dowse.

Allow at least a three-day interval between the preparation exercise, and actual dowsing. During this time you should feel your confidence and new energy developing for your dowsing experiment. You are the source, you have the power and ability to be successful at dowsing. It's just a matter of accepting this fact that makes it all possible. You must believe in your own esoteric ability and with patience, belief and practice you will soon enjoy the results of dowsing.

THE DOWSING EXPERIENCE

After the preparation days and up to the dowsing day, continually reinforce your inner strength by repeating your Edict.

On the day you start your first dowsing work, dress lightly and protect your head from the sun if necessary. A venture like this can be quite exciting when you work closely with someone else. You can exchange ideas and one can record while the other is dowsing. Stay as calm and relaxed as possible. Remember, dowsing is a natural gift that you have not yet experienced. You are learning to avail yourself of energy and power that, until now, you were possibly not aware of.

If possible, enjoy you experiment with an experienced dowser who can help you translate the many subtle signs of dowsing. An experienced dowser learns how to respond to the many different signs and indications that a novice could easily overlook.

If you are working with a companion who is also inexperienced, you can learn together. Select a place that is quiet and secluded. Place the divining rod on the ground with your Edict and have a few quiet moments before you begin. Focus your mind on your inner power and let the divining rod and the Edict fuse together with your purpose.

You are now ready to slowly explore the area you have chosen. Hold the divining rod out before you and be aware of any movement. No matter how slight, pause, and see how the movement develops. Have your companion make a note of all movements and the exact area in which they occur. Receiving a slight movement may indicate guidance from the Higher Self. After pausing, slowly step forward and then come back. Now slowly move a step to the right and come back again. Repeat the same movements to your left. If your divining rod responds, then follow that particular direction, still moving slowly. Fast movements will prevent you from receiving the slight impulses from the divining rod. Be acutely aware and follow the signs of the rod. Continue exploring.

A strong pull or jerk indicates an area to definitely investigate. Your Edict will determine how you should explore further. As you develop your dowsing skill, you will need more sophisticated pieces of equipment. A tool to dig with, something to kneel on, a camera, perhaps, and a suitable bag or container to collect your findings.

After your first dowsing expedition lie all kinds of interesting and specialized areas. You will probably want to contact a good organization that can help you with additional information. Essentially, you are exploring your own input of power—learning to recognize its existence and then applying a conscious effort to use and control it. You may never become an expert dowser, but you can certainly learn how it works and enjoy the anticipation of finding something hidden by using your own inner power.

THE PENDULUM

In the same field of expression we have the pendulum. One form of the pendulum is, in fact, the divining rod. The same type of energy is involved. The difference is that the pendulum can be used indoors, whereas dowsing is essentially an outdoor activity. Both are based on the theory that the power is within you, and not the instrument used.

A pendulum is a small weight, suspended on a chain, cord or thread. It is used for various esoteric practices. It can be used in dowsing as a diagnostic implement. Some dowsers use a pendulum when searching for certain minerals, water and oil. Experienced users of pendulums have a variety of beautiful pendants. Some are quite exotic and become symbolic to the user. Choosing your personal pendulum is similar to selecting a key chain. It's a matter of preference. The more unusual the pendant, the more esoteric it can become to the user.

For the purpose of testing your pendulum skill, you can use any type of pendant. A house key or a large bead will be fine. The cord or chain should be no shorter than twelve inches and no longer than eighteen. A strong steady arm, a notepad and pen, plus a good helping of patience are the only other ingredients.

The first step is to find your own basic way to communicate via the pendulum using a simple "Yes" and "No" system. Defining such a "code" is important, otherwise you are not going to know what the pendulum movements mean. Although many people are convinced that a straight back-and-forth movement means one thing, and a round circular movement means another, the fact is that it may differ for each individual.

The pendulum is an esoteric tool. You are the source of power and energy. You are the channel for this energy to come through. So first of all, do an initial test and, as always before participating in esoteric procedures, shed White Light around you.

Write something on a piece of paper and have someone else write the same thing on a separate piece of paper. Hold the chain of the pendulum over your original piece of paper and allow the bottom of the pendulum to gently touch the paper for a moment. Now ask, "Did I write this?" Wait until the pendulum starts to move in a definite pattern, and make a note of this pattern—for example, in a circle, or back and forth. Remove the original writing and replace it with the other. Ask the same question and, once again, note the movement of your pendulum. If your result is two separate movements, then you have established your own personal "Yes" and "No" code.

Continuing now as with your initial test, you can determine your personal code for "Male" and "Female." Clear the table and ask another simple question "Am I male or female?" Note the type of movement. Your second question might be to ask about someone of the opposite sex. When you receive two different movements, you are developing your personal code of communication.

Sometimes it takes a little while before you begin to have a response. I guarantee that if you are patient you will soon be able to work with the pendulum. There are many simple test exercises you can do. For example, put an envelope on the table and ask if the letter comes from a "Male" or "Female." Ask if it is raining outside and see if your "Yes" and "No" system is still intact. Receiving assurance on these simple questions will enable you to ask questions of a more serious nature. It's a good idea to write down a simple list of questions requiring a "Yes" or "No," and also "Male" and "Female" answers. Once you are sure of your skill with these, you can progress further.

When the questions become serious and the answers have been tested and proven, the student becomes curious. Much is said and written about psychic phenomena, yet there is a tendency to skirt the main issue. As long as there is a sense of personal command and control, it is plainly acceptable. On the other hand, when we receive intelligent communication and information that would not normally be known, then it becomes a problem unless the source is identified.

All activities preceded with White Light and a serious approach should be registered in an ongoing Psychic Journal of Development. To eliminate doubt and fear, you should always acknowledge the true source, which has its origin within the Universal Force. Your intent, integrity and sincerity will not only protect you from negativity, but also attract the level you are seeking.

Always, *always*, recognize yourself as the pure source. Like attracts like, so therefore you can receive information past, present and future as seen from your Higher Self. It is also possible that you can go beyond that esoteric point. In your desire to seek truth and wisdom, your Higher Self may pierce the pure levels of the Master. Then the information received form this high level may come in the form of advice and/or guidance.

The Master level is separate from the Higher Consciousness. To connect with this higher level, you have to approach through your own individual spirituality—that is, through self, going directly into your own power, which gives access to a higher spiritual realm. On this level, highly evolved souls exist and the Higher Self can obtain a higher level of spiritual guidance.

When we speak of angels, guides and Masters, we are referring to this higher level of spiritual existence. In recognizing our own spiritual source, we can reach a peak of personal spirituality devoid of all worldly concern. This is your soul, the real you, no longer confined to physical or material matters. The strength and purity of true self is the soul that enters life after life in search of spiritual perfection and the refinement of existence.

The Higher Self can freely approach the Master level. The spiritual entity of the Master level is often personalized and recognized by the Higher Self as a further source of wisdom.

This Master source of wisdom has access to all knowledge. The Higher Self can communicate with the Master level and convey its findings to the Conscious level. Because the Conscious level has the need to know the source, the Higher Self relates this intelligence to it from the Master level. To allow the Conscious level to know the difference, the Higher Self determines and then identifies the higher source. As parents give a child a name, so does the Higher Self give a name to a spiritual envoy responsible for the source of wisdom and knowledge. This name is recognized by the Conscious level as an angel, guide or Master.

THE ESOTERIC LINE

This whole process need not remain a mystery to the serious student. When the true source of spirituality becomes a realistic goal, then each level of learning is easily identified. There is a line of esoteric communication. Following this line allows your Conscious mind to understand the spiritual function of the esoteric levels.

THE FORMAT

1. Recognize your own source of spirituality. Know that you have continuous strength and power.

2. Always protect yourself in White Light. This takes you immediately to your personal source.

3. From this source you have access to your Higher Self.

4. The Higher Self has access to the higher levels of spiritual existence, where wisdom and knowledge may be obtained. We refer to this source as the Master level.

5. On the Master level, the Higher Self can communicate with evolved souls who give guidance and assistance for the Conscious level on earth.

6. To help the Conscious level understand the spiritual source, the Higher Self identifies and names the spiritual contact.

7. This spiritual envoy is usually recognized as an angel, guide or Master.

In summary, recognize your own spiritual source; reach to the Higher Self, through self; ask for the spiritual identity of the incoming information and be satisfied with the verification received.

This format is not limited to one particular aspect of psychic research. In all areas of unknown or unfamiliar means of communication, this format should be considered. If a person rang your front doorbell you would want to know why he was there. After he gave you a reason you might require further information—his name and identification. These same assurances are necessary on all esoteric levels. Never take anything for granted, and always verify.

We can see that, through self, one is able to communicate with the various spiritual levels. Although pomp and ceremony are not necessary, discipline is! You enter your own spiritual path of discipline through White Light, then, as the Conscious mind opens to the esoteric levels, it must satisfy its own curiosity and intellect.

Therefore, the Conscious mind will form a pattern of inquiry, establishing its authenticity with each step. There is no one method. Each individual works with what he feels is spiritually substantial and satisfying. Because of these inner needs for security, man through the centuries has formulated procedures or prerequisite rituals as guidelines and steps, to go beyond "normal" patterns of thinking and communicating.

Whether working with a pendulum or any other type of Divination, you should approach "through self." Never be afraid to ask for further information. If, for example, you are given the name "Jack," it is quite in order to ask for the last name also. Always question the source of information received. Your Higher Self will be alert to the source, and it will also let you know if you are being influenced by your Conscious level. If you feel doubtful or unsatisfied, come back to your source and the White Light, and begin again.

Ritual, or formulated patterns of conducting your psychic research or Divination, are really personal steps of confidence on your spiritual path of discipline. They become habitual and important. As each step takes you to the next step, you feel confidence as you fulfill your self-imposed format or rules. Other people's rituals can feel uncomfortable, simply because you don't necessarily have the same needs. Ritual is like dress—it is very personal, and one style does not always suit another.

The White Light can be considered a part of your personal formula. It represents protection, purity of intent, and the desire to reach spiritual levels of wisdom and understanding. Whatever way you create White Light becomes important. When your mind has it firmly established, this will be the only way that feels right. The way you approach your inner spirituality is the key to the Higher Self. Without this key, you may feel unable to reach your own higher wisdom.

CHAPTER FIFTEEN

TUNING INWARD

Testing yourself assures the Conscious mind that it is possible to receive information from a higher source. Once you convince yourself, then you will gain the confidence to share your ability with others. To begin a self-testing process, you do not need to use any particular Divination procedure. A self-test is like psychic "push-ups." Many interesting things occur daily! You have already learned to merge both Conscious and psychic thought patterns. Through the years, you have developed an automatic skill that enables you to extract knowledge from two sources, or levels. Once you obtain the information you need, it is channelled directly through the Conscious mind. What has happened is that, in your need or quest for knowledge, you searched the Conscious level; if the answer was unavailable, then you automatically probed your psychic center. This whole process is completed so swiftly that you are not always aware of just how you obtained the information.

To conduct a personal test, you must learn to rely entirely on your psychic center. It is a simple process and can be quite enjoyable. Next time the phone rings, stop for a moment, and see if you can tell who is calling you. Another simple self-test is to try and tell yourself the time of day. Before you do, stop for a moment and allow your psychic center to work for you. Before long you will be able to accomplish these simple processes. Without looking at your mail, handle each piece separately

117

and see if you can tell who it is from. The next time you misplace something at home or in the office, stop for a moment and see if you can psychically obtain its location.

There are many ways in which you can test yourself. Don't give up—keep trying, and soon you will see improvement. This helps you learn to rely on your own psychic center. At first it might be difficult. Your Conscious mind may feel insecure. But with practice, you will learn to ignore the doubt of the Conscious level.

Since you already use a certain amount of psychic skill, by self-testing you will soon realize how much. From this point on, you can develop new ways of self-testing. On nine pieces of paper, each approximately three inches square, write the numbers one through nine. Turn them over and see if you are able to guess which is which correctly. Touch is an invaluable aid to this type of testing. Allowing your fingers to touch the paper can help tremendously. You can, of course, use ordinary playing cards or purchase special cards designed for Psychic Development.

It is not a question of whether or not you have a psychic center—everyone does! Just as we all have a physical body, of a particular shape and size, so we all have a psychic center. With good esoteric exercise, you can learn to develop a higher ratio of sensitivity. I have mentioned a few simple self-tests and this is a good way to begin your own Psychic Development. Learning how you actually respond, and in which way, gives you a good starting point.

REACTING TO COLOR

Color lends its influence to everyone and everything. Color determines attitude and mood, depending on your personal receptivity. Behavior patterns are influenced by surrounding colors. Each individual is affected in a different way, depending on the impact a specific color may have on him.

As soon as we think of color, we respond on varying levels of Consciousness. Color is a part of nature, flowers, plants and trees. The change of seasons has an enormous impact on us. Even now, as you read, you are forming sweeping changes of color in your mental image. Animals vary not only in size, but in color also, and they rely on color for many things—mating, hunting, etc. The beauty and majesty of life is presented in a magnificent variety of color. We feel the impact of color in dress, food, home and work conditions. Every room in the house is important and the colors in a particular room will either enhance the activity or oppose it.

Violet, indigo and blue are colors at one end of the spectrum. They make good background colors and each of them should be considered in association with the expected activity of the room. At the other end of the color spectrum we have red, orange and yellow. These three colors are good for accents, as they have a longer vibratory pattern. They are more physical. Violet, indigo and blue have a shorter vibratory pattern, and they have a more relaxing effect. Green is the mid-color on the spectrum and adds strength and stability toward the opposing color sequences.

The individual response to color differs. That is why, for example, green is not everyone's favorite color! This individual receptivity originates from our personal color structures. Each color has its own internal spectrum, also, from its very lightest shade to its deepest tones. Within one color alone there are many subtle shades that are comfortable and complementary to the inner esoteric structure or possibly cause a sense of disharmony and unbalance. The sensitivity to color begins at birth, so you can see how important it is to be aware of the supporting or non-supporting energies of the colors that surround us.

Color is either complementary or abrasive to the delicate esoteric structures. Governed by the two separate nervous systems, man responds to life and his surroundings through a complex series of physical, mental and spiritual impulses. The involuntary nervous system is so designed that it has an automatic function providing what is necessary for the physical body. This includes the breathing mechanism, the heart, vital fluids and digestive system. The other system, which is a voluntary process, has its central point in the brain. This second system governs our capacity to think, and to be aware of feelings that initiate any action we take.

Color affects our metabolism on all levels, Conscious or otherwise. The intriguing effect of color can also stimulate the higher Conscious level. The power of color can accelerate the lifting of Consciousness, as in meditation. Although you may feel oblivious to color, every aspect of your being is exposed to the vibratory patterns that color generates.

If the vibratory influences of color are conducive to the delicate esoteric structure, this creates a sense of well-being. Too much or too little color can influence the esoteric balance accordingly. You may dislike something as simple as a dress or a shirt for no other reason than its color; likewise, a room or a painting. Once you reject a color, a message is sent directly to the Conscious level and you may find yourself opposed to something that you might ordinarily like if the color were different.

COLORED CANDLES

Lighting colored candles releases a strong impact of color vibrations. The flame represents light, life and energy. When a candle is lighted, it gives out a continuous flow of energy, which is determined by the actual color of the candle. Feeling good indicates that you are receiving the right type of energy. This enhances your meditation and you will be appreciative and receptive when the particular energy is supportive to your esoteric needs.

The vibratory flow created by lighting a candle can be quite exhilarating. Each color lends its own supportive energy.

DEGREES OF COLOR

Each color has its own ratio of expression, and there are many subtle shades of each color. Think of Red, letting your mind visualize the very lightest shade of Red. Now picture in your mind the deepest and darkest shade of Red and you will not only realize the difference but you can actually feel it.

(If you find it difficult to visualize the subtle shades of color, you can use other means to conduct your personal color test. Visit your local paint or hardware store and get a color card showing various shades for each color. Any store that sells artists' supplies can provide you with colored pencils, or other information pertinent to color.)

Now take the color Green. Green represents foundations, discipline and order. A person might avoid exercising these qualities, or over-exercise them. In either case, we could recognize the actual use of the vibratory flow by the resulting color tone. We might see a lighter shade of green or a deeper shade of green. Each color has its own vibratory sequence. Depending on the circumstances, a person may vacillate up and down the color frequency, representing a feeling of instability or unbalance. Another example might be a person who constantly operates only on the lighter tones. This would suggest that the person has some difficulty in establishing his true personality. The other extreme would be someone who exists solely on the deeper tones, presenting a dominant personality.

These examples represent extreme situations. The average person fluctuates on his own vibratory scale of expression. The law of karma is quite evident when we analyze how the natal numerical chart converts to the color spectrum. The original natal structure indicates exactly how the soul intended to live this particular life. It does not require an in-depth study to see the esoteric purpose in relation to the color structure that the name gives.

In the following chart are the seven rainbow colors, and their positive and negative expressions. Seldom would anyone function under a continuously extreme positive or negative influence; usually it is the subtler forms of these influences that become a noticeable part of the personality.

COLOR		POSITIVE EXPRESSION	NEGATIVE EXPRESSION
RED	=	INDIVIDUALITY	SELFISHNESS
ORANGE	=	COOPERATION	SELF-PITY
YELLOW	=	SELF-EXPRESSION	CONCEIT
GREEN	=	DISCIPLINE	PROCRASTINATION
BLUE	=	FREEDOM	SELF-INDULGENCE
INDIGO	=	BALANCE	CHAOS
VIOLET	=	INNER WISDOM	IGNORANCE

FOOD AND COLOR

Food can also contribute to the esoteric balance. Sometimes the foods necessary to an individual may be disliked. Esoterically, it is good to eat foods that are complementary to your natal structure—especially if you feel out of sorts.

Regardless of *how* color is used in life, it works! Too much, too little—be it food, clothes or décor, it adds or detracts from our personal spiritual balance. Difficult though it may seem, breakfast actually sets the scene for our daily activities. For example, a glass of orange juice followed by eggs and coffee gives an immediate dose of color energy when your day begins.

ORANGE JUICE provides a perfect input of pure orange, which helps you to be cooperative and considerate of others.

EGGS provide stimulation to the emotional level, as they increase the vibratory flow of yellow. This enables you to be expressive without fear or reservation.

COFFEE also provides substance to the emotional level, and gives the stimuli needed for creativity and expression.

All foods should be considered in terms of esoteric need. Food categories of red, orange and yellow all contribute toward an increase in energy—not only physical, but also mental and spiritual.

Too much or too little of each category will increase or decrease the type of energy you personally require. Everyone has their own specific needs. A well-balanced color diet that is excellent for you may not necessarily work for your partner. The following exercise is designed to help you categorize foods. See how many items you normally eat in each group. Then analyze these food preferences.

As you categorize your regular choice of foods into the color groups, you will see how your diet has become part of your personality. "You are what you eat" is an old saying and very true! If you find you are missing an entire color sequence, this will be recognized in your personality, efforts and goals.

EXERCISE 15: ESOTERIC FOOD GROUPS

COLOR	SAMPLE FOODS	YOUR OWN FOOD PREFERENCES
RED	Tomatoes, beets	_____
ORANGE	Carrots, oranges	_____

YELLOW   Lemons, bananas   _____

GREEN   Beans, lettuce   _____

BLUE   Grapes, blueberries   _____

INDIGO   Includes foods from   _____
          BLUE and VIOLET.

VIOLET   Eggplant, blackberries   _____

CHAPTER SIXTEEN

TUNING OUTWARD

As you learn to tune inward you assimilate esoteric knowledge. Once you absolutely "know" how this information works for you on a personal level, then you can begin to "tune outward." Observe how the esoteric law works for everyone. Realize that the Universal power is available to all. It works in exactly the same way for all. As with mathematics, once you learn the essential laws governing the subject, you can make all manner of computations. The basic laws of math always remain the same, like "two and two equal four." The more you learn, the more you will know.

Applying esoteric law increases your spirituality and also provides you with the stamina needed to accomplish your life path. The more you learn, the more you will recognize how rarely the karmic laws are practiced. The law of karma is the law of cause and effect. So it is vital to establish some well-defined causes. Once you do this, esoteric law will provide the effects.

Observe how those around you maintain balance. See how easily balance can be lost by yourself and others. Be alert to the karmic laws, and know that every act of breaking down situations and relationships is followed by the need to rebuild. This karmic law is natural and it acts automatically. We cannot fight the harmony and balance of the Universal laws. That being so, it behooves us all to respect these laws, and make constant effort to retain our personal equilibrium in all things.

When an esoteric scholar reaches a certain level of knowledge and understanding, he learns to ignore the defense mechanisms of man and directs his attention at all times to his own spiritual nature. Using unnecessary energies to defend, control and assert the ego has a devastating effect on the very thing you are trying to protect. Your own relationship with God is your responsibility. Rather than fight the negativity of others, it is far better to contribute toward the apparent deficiencies. Prayer for healing on physical, mental and spiritual levels will benefit all parties concerned.

Tune outward, and realize that the struggle and dilemmas you see are trapped within the limitations of the ego. Until you take action, it is difficult to let go of egotistical ties. Learn how to replace false securities and be willing to release the old and boldly accept new ways of accomplishing tired goals.

COMING INTO YOUR PSYCHIC CENTER

Imagine the physical body as a house with many rooms. In one of these rooms is your Psychic Center. Some people have ready access to their own Psychic Center. Others may be surprised to know of its existence. How you feel about your Psychic Center has no bearing on the fact that it not only exists but that you can locate this unique esoteric area.

Taking the analogy further, imagine that the door to your Psychic Center is closed. It is located "upstairs," on a Higher level. You need an answer, and from behind the closed door you can faintly hear a voice—but you are unable to detect what it is saying. Rather than go up to the room and open the door, you might choose to find an alternate way of dealing with your situation!

Yet within the confines of your Psychic Center are marvelous and astounding tools of life. It may seem so much quicker to find alternate ways to solve a current situation, but once you locate the correct solving mechanism you will find that lingering and repeated dilemmas do not recur. Once a problem is dealt with correctly, it cannot seed future problems.

THE INNER WORKINGS

It is not really difficult to acknowledge the existence of your own Psychic Center. Think about the five senses of man: hearing, seeing, tasting, smelling and touching.

To hear, see, taste, smell or touch requires an inner activity of the body. In a flash, we can avail ourselves of all five senses. For example, while drinking a cup of good, strong coffee we might hear a voice. As the speaker comes closer, we might smell a familiar perfume. We could turn toward the direction of the voice and see someone we know. To acknowledge the status of the relationship we might hug or shake hands. In such a brief moment, you would have used all the senses of man.

You can develop a sixth sense by exercising your personal Psychic Center. There are many, many ways in which you can approach inner development. Some methods of Divination can automatically connect one with the Psychic Center.

Certain Divination procedures alert the higher senses, which allows immediate access to the Psychic Center. Meditation is an excellent way to open up and develop the sixth sense. There are those who are gifted and seem born with a highly developed sixth sense. But remember, an Olympic athlete is not born with running shoes or a javelin! It takes concentration, continued effort, patience and in-depth training to reach an Olympic standard. The same is true of Psychic Development.

If you are prepared to train diligently, like an Olympic athlete, you will attain a high standard of skill. It all begins with the *wanting*. You must *want* to achieve a high standard, and be prepared to work towards your goal. Then you can be assured that you will gain the results you intend. This takes more than reading a book. It requires the application of what you read, study and learn to open your Psychic Center. At some point you may want to find a teacher who will help you achieve the levels you seek. When this happens you must be sure to locate the right teacher—someone who understands your needs and will work with you to achieve the spiritual standards you have set for yourself. A good teacher will guide you and be with you as you journey on your spiritual path.

EXERCISE 16: DISCOVER YOUR VIBRATORY FREQUENCY

All esoteric exercises and/or meditations require loose clothing. If possible, wear WHITE. But in this exercise it is *necessary* to wear WHITE, to establish a neutral esoteric position. If you are wearing any color, it will prevent you from receiving the information you need.

You will need seven pieces of cloth—handkerchiefs or scarves are perfect for this exercise. The type of material does not matter, though silk is ideal. When using silk you become more acutely aware of the vibratory frequency. I recommend that counselors and teachers use silk, to ensure that the esoteric process is both accurate and satisfactory.

The physical, mental and spiritual benefits gained through this exercise may prompt you to obtain seven rainbow pieces of silk, so you can use this exercise optimally to determine your needs on the color frequency daily, weekly or monthly.

This exercise requires two people. Be sure you have a partner who can be sufficiently serious to enable you to conduct this esoteric test.

The person undergoing the test is Person A.

The person conducting the test is Person B.

PERSON A

1. Person A is to be dressed in WHITE loose clothing with no jewelry whatsoever.

2. Person A should be standing on something WHITE. This can be a WHITE tablecloth or rug, or a large piece of white paper.

3. Stand with feet slightly apart and eyes *closed*. This is to ensure that the response is clear, and void of any thought energy.

4. Arms should be down and held slightly away from the body, with hands stretched open.

PERSON B

1. Person B should also be dressed in WHITE with no jewelry whatsoever. Any color worn by Person B will in some way affect the results of the esoteric exercise.

2. Stand five or six feet away from Partner A, making sure he is standing correctly, with eyes closed.

3. Ask your partner to visualize WHITE energy all around. Now ask your partner to inhale three WHITE energy breaths.

4. Now say, "As I count to seven, relax and feel the WHITE energy surrounding you." Count out loud, slowly, to seven.

5. Have your rainbow cloths ready. Select the one you want to use first.

6. Ask Parner A to stretch out his left arm. Place the cloth lightly in his hand.

7. Place your right hand on Partner A's upper arm above the elbow, and ask your partner to offer resistance as you now press his arm down toward the side of his body.

8. Do this three times and observe the resistance or lack of resistance from Partner A. Remember that during this whole testing process Partner A should have his eyes *closed*.

9. Now take the cloth from Partner A's left hand and place it in his right hand. Conduct the same test, pushing the right arm three times and observing the reaction.

10. Continue the test in the same way with each of the cloths. Allow a short time between each color so that Partner A may regain his inner balance before each color test.

TEST OBSERVATIONS

After going through the seven colors have Partner A sit on the WHITE material on the floor, and relax for a few moments.

The effects of this test can be quite surprising. You can tell by the measure of resistance which colors are strong, weak, normal, or nonexistent.

Taking notes is important and understanding the notes is even more important! To have a clear reference for the test take a piece of paper and make the following column headings.

Beginning at the far left hand side of the paper, your first column should read "COLOR." In this column, write the color you were testing. Then write the rest of the column headings.

Column 1: Color being tested

Column 2: No Resistance

Column 3: Very Weak

Column 4: Weak

Column 5: Medium

Column 6: Medium/Strong

Column 7: Strong

Column 8: Total Resistance

Before commencing the test select the order of colors and write them in Column 1. As you conduct each test make your decision a result of applying energy three times. Just make a check mark in the column of your choice before proceeding to the next color.

TEST RESULTS

The results of testing the Color Frequency can vary in several ways, depending on how intricate you want to be. The result of the test shows a deficiency or strength in any particular color sequence, but the reasons could be many. As we look at the result headings we might see "weak" checked off for the color Red. This would indicate that Partner A—*at this time*—does not have a sufficient measure of INDIVIDUALITY.

Note that I said *at this time*! If, for example, a person is undergoing stress at work, home or in a relationship they might possibly have a "weak" reaction to Red. When our individuality is threatened in any way, then we lose a measure of the Red vibratory sequence. On the other hand, if the test reaction were TOTAL RESISTANCE, this could be for many different reasons. The person may have a domineering personality or at this particular time in life be undergoing pressures which force him to assert his individuality.

The test may be continued by analyzing the results and applying a color remedy. If we discover a deficiency in Red, a simple remedy might be to wear more Red, meditate with Red candles, and eat foods in the Red category.

During this self-balancing process, be sensitive to any changes regarding health, attitude and personality. Of course, any question about health requires a medical doctor. These tests can enhance and improve, but they do not replace medical advice.

To make your test more interesting, make a note of the date. Try to increase your exposure to any colors your test indicates are deficient. If you find a strong resistance to a particular color, modify your use of, or exposure to, that color. In about a week, make a new test and see if you have improved your Color Frequency.

The color of your bedding generates a vibratory effect while you sleep. You are also susceptible to the color of the car you drive, especially the interior color.

If you find your car is not totally compatible with your needs I don't suggest you sell the car! Just by wearing the color, you will modify any surrounding colors. The awareness of color in your life will fortify the energy around you. By using specific colors you will improve your ability to reach goals and your lifestyle in general.

STABILIZING FREQUENCY STRUCTURE

Color is a vital part of your esoteric balance. The varying shades of light and dark can be renewed and stabilized. The frequency structure is a myriad of vital color that governs the equilibrium. There is no universal pattern—everyone has his own unique frequency structure.

The human aura is a reflection of esoteric activity combined with sensitivity. Unless these personal energies are aligned and balanced, we become adversely affected in some way. The Higher Self continually reminds other levels of Consciousness of any disturbance or intrusion that causes the frequency structure any stress. To an insensitive person, this message from the Higher Self might be considered frustration or discontent.

The Conscious mind darts here and there, experiencing life as it happens. The Higher Consciousness has extended vision and can see clearly the karmic path ahead. The actual level of sensitivity determines the nature of contact between these two Consciousness levels. (The subconscious is busy recording all that happens!)

Here we see a vital link between the Conscious level and the Higher Consciousness. Imagine two people holding hands. One person has his head turned and is looking into the distance. The second person is steadily gazing directly at the other. There is a close binding with hands holding, yet one man looks away and the other tries to attract his attention. Here we have a simplified idea of the two Conscious levels.

The following exercise is designed to help the Higher Consciousness get the attention of the Conscious level. The exercise procedure will certainly achieve this, but not necessarily contain this esoteric communication. The key to maintaining a permanent tie is within the Conscious level. It is a direct and forthright effort to recognize the joy and contentment that can be yours when you purposely direct Conscious thoughts, needs and actions to the Higher Consciousness.

THE SUPPORT OF NEGATIVITY

Negativity is often a crutch—a support—holding on to situations, relationships, etc., simply because one cannot see an alternative. Sad though this may be, it is so. One of the strongest negative support systems is saying, "There is nothing I can do about it." Many precious years are wasted as we lean on negative support. Oddly enough, somewhere, sometime in life a person comes along or a situation occurs, and in the force of the new circumstance, we let go!

In letting go, new and wonderful supports are available. We become enchanted, and perhaps overwhelmed, with the many choices before us. Unfortunately, we often feel we must wait for something to happen. Of course, this is not true. Each of us stands at the helm of our own life.

The Conscious level is eager to make quick decisions. It needs to know and feel the comfort of routine. The Higher Self needs time to communicate and fill the Conscious level with new ideas and plans. In this state of "not knowing," the Conscious level feels insecure and will often grab at the first support system it can find—regardless of whether it is good, bad or indifferent. Then the empty feeling and sensitivity that occur during what should be a time of communication between the two levels are closed off. The first step to changing this is to anticipate the void and accept that within this void there is a high level of spiritual communication. Preparing for this spiritual shift requires letting go of fear—all kinds of fear. Allow and permit yourself time to open up your Higher Consciousness.

To renew and stabilize, the esoteric scholar must first work diligently with the Conscious level. There are many surprises! How receptive you have been to the input of negativity will determine how quickly you can successfully establish your renewal and stabilization. Many of the doubts and fears are still tied to the subconscious.

In the next exercise, you will recognize the support systems—both positive and negative. You will discover their foundations and how they were originally rooted. You will look beyond the confining obstacles of everyday life and view the karmic path ahead. You will feel the release of negativity as you recognize the inner need to make changes. Your goal is to experience the true joy of being in command of your life.

PREPARATION FOR EXERCISES 17 AND 18

The next exercises renew and stabilize your esoteric structure. The nature of these two exercises is both beneficial and spiritually rewarding—bringing yourself to the very center of who you really are. From this place you find a new and exciting strength. In the discovery of "self," your esoteric ability increases, allowing you an objective look at your life path, the power to rearrange it, and the joy of making new, meaningful goals.

1. Dress loosely, and only wear jewelry that is special to you.

2. For exercise 17, place seven WHITE candles on a table before you.

3. For exercise 18, place seven WHITE candles on the table, and seven colored candles—one in each color of the rainbow*— immediately behind the WHITE candles.

4. Have pen and paper available on the table.

5. Use a vase of fresh flowers when possible. Place it in the center back of the table.

6. Place a chair at the table.

7. Place two glasses of water on the table, left and right.

EXERCISE 17: SPIRITUAL ANALYSIS

1. Standing before the table, say:
   "I ask for clarity and the vision to see what I must do. I ask sincerely for help and strength. As I come into the Universal Light, I ask a blessing for all those in need and all those I love. Amen."

2. Lighting the first candle (behind it is the RED candle) say:
   "I recognize the power of God. I light this pure white candle in honor and love. I ask that my individuality be balanced according to my spiritual journey. I relinquish my fears of all earthly things. I ask that my soul be renewed and purified. I pray that the flame will purify and strengthen my true individuality. I release all false ego, I release all that has prevented me from standing within Thy Holy eternal Light. Amen."

3. Now sit and write clearly *all* the aspects of your individuality that you consider *no longer useful*. If you encounter any difficulty, put the pen down and ask for help as you look at the flame. Remember the flame is your spiritual inspiration.

---

*Red, Orange, Yellow, Green, Blue, Indigo, Purple

4. When you are finished, fold the paper in half, twice, and place it before the lighted candle, saying:
   "I have honestly tried to rid myself of all negativity that has crushed my true individuality. I now gaze into the divine flame and I know my soul is renewed. Amen."

5. Once again, stand before the table and say:
   "I ask for clarity and the vision to see what I must do. I ask sincerely for help and strength. As I come into the Universal Light I ask a blessing for all those in need and all those I love. Amen."

6. Lighting the second candle (behind it is the ORANGE candle), say:
   "I recognize the power of God. I light this pure white candle in honor and love. I ask that all my relationships be put into proper perspective. I ask for a deeper understanding of my spiritual obligations and my obligations to others. If I unknowingly have been selfish, non-caring, harsh, bitter, unrelenting, or unappreciative I ask now, dear Father, that all these things be taken from me. Help me to see all my relationships in Thy Divine Light. Please give me insight so that I can see who I am in all my relationships. I ask for strength to correct and balance all of my ties. Release my fears so that I may do what is right and just for all. Amen."

7. Sit down and write clearly *all* the aspects of your relationships that you consider need help, improvement, severance, reestablishing, understanding, etc. If you encounter any difficulty, put the pen down and ask for help as you look into the flame of the second WHITE candle. This exercise takes time; don't try to rush things. Take each step with spiritual care.

8. When you have finished your writing, fold the paper in half twice, and place it before the lighted candle, saying:
   "I have truly tried to rid myself of all negativity that has jeopardized my relationships. I now gaze into the divine flame and I know my soul is renewed. Amen."

9. Standing before the table, say:
   "I ask for clarity and the vision to see what I must do. I ask

sincerely for help and strength. As I come into the Universal Light I ask a blessing for all those in need and all those I love. Amen."

10. Lighting the third candle (behind it is the YELLOW candle), say:
"I recognize the power of God. I light this pure white candle in honor and love. I ask that my creative energy be positive and rewarding on all levels. Let me not be too concerned with myself. Help me to direct my thoughts to those around me. Help me, dear Father, to be ever-considerate of others. Let me not knowingly hurt or prevent anyone from being themselves. I ask that I may use my creativity with a great measure of consideration. As I build my life and walk upon my life path, let me not hinder, hurt or prevent anyone else from doing the same. Give me the courage, dear Father, to do all the things I must do. I ask for Thy holy presence to be with me in my efforts, work and joy. You have given me many gifts. Let me always be aware of Thy love and blessings. Amen."

11. Sit now and write clearly all the wonderful gifts and blessings that you have. In your writing, acknowledge what has been given you. Describe how you are using your talents. Include the creativity and talent that you misuse. If you encounter any difficulty, put the pen down and ask for help as you look into the flame. Make an effort to see all the blessings and talent you have. As you look into the flame, try to see how you can fulfill your true destiny.

12. When you have considered all these things, fold the paper in half twice and place it before the lighted candle, saying:
"I have tried, dear Father, to see the many gifts and talents you have given me. From this day on, I will try to use them and glorify Thy Holy Name. Amen."

13. Standing again by the table, say:
"I ask for clarity and vision to see what I must do. I ask sincerely for help and strength. As I come into the Universal Light I ask a blessing for all those in need and all those I love. Amen."

14. Lighting the fourth candle (behind it is the GREEN candle), say:

    "I recognize the power of God. I light this pure white candle in honor and love. I ask that my foundations be firm and well-rooted in self-discipline. I am ever grateful for the power you have given me. Teach me, Father, to use it well and with concern for everyone. I ask for the wisdom to remove all undesirable situations I have built. I come to you as a child and ask You, Father, to help me build all that is good and beneficial. I will remove all my fear and make new foundations from the love and wisdom You have given me. Amen."

15. Sit once more and write clearly *all* the foundations you have put in your life. Examine the growth, acknowledge the love and pleasures of life. Have courage to observe past errors. If you encounter any difficulty, put the pen down and ask for help as you look in the flame. Look to new horizons of possibility and do not dwell on past failures.

16. After you have finished writing, fold the paper in half twice and place it before the lighted candle, saying:

    "I have looked well into the many foundations I have laid. I have seen the situations and circumstances I have built. Some are good, dear Father, some are not. Help me at this time to begin in a new positive way. I now gaze into the divine flame and I know my soul is renewed. Amen."

17. Now stand and say:

    "I ask for clarity and vision to see what I must do. I ask sincerely for help and strength. As I come into the Universal Light I ask a blessing for all those in need and all those I love. Amen."

18. Lighting the fifth candle (behind it is the BLUE candle), say:

    "I recognize the power of God. I light this pure WHITE candle in honor and in love. I pray for divine guidance to help me discover and explore my inner need for freedom. I pray to release myself from all negativity, knowing full well that beyond my negativity is my spiritual freedom. I pray for this gift for myself and others. Dear Father, whatever binds me to my fear, I ask that You release me in Thy divine wisdom. Amen."

19. Sit again and write clearly regarding your restrictions and the type of freedom you need in your life. Be prepared to see reality. Acknowledge self-made barriers. Look beyond these obstacles and see the wonder and beauty of the freedom you crave. If you encounter any difficulty, put the pen down and ask for help as you look in the flame. Know that within the flame is the wisdom and the key to the freedom of expression you desire.

20. When you have finished writing, fold the paper in half twice and place before the lighted candle, saying:
"Dear Father, I have tried to pierce all barriers of negativity and fear. I know these things have prevented me from experiencing true spiritual freedom. I now gaze into the divine flame and I know my soul is renewed. Amen."

21. Now stand and say:
"I ask for clarity and vision to see what I must do. I ask sincerely for help and strength. As I come into the Universal Light I ask a blessing for all those in need and all those I love. Amen."

22. Lighting the sixth candle (behind it is the INDIGO candle), say:
"I recognize the power of God. I light this pure white candle in honor and love. I ask for peace, tranquillity, balance and harmony on all levels of Consciousness. I pray that my inner vision will be opened so that I may see what I must do in this life. Often I feel alone, dear Father, but I know Thy presence is always with me. When I am lost and afraid, may the divine Light of Thy glory show me the way. Hear my voice as I cry in the darkness of my own dilemma. Open my eyes so that I might see the beauty and wonder of life. Help me to retain my spiritual balance in all things. As a child I ask to come home and never leave the glory of Thy love. Amen."

23. Sitting now, start to write clearly your deepest needs. Recognize why your life becomes so complex. See how your spiritual balance has been affected over and over again with the same

type of situations. See where and how you make mistakes and ask for help in future situations. Look at your life and see how the tranquillity of God can once again fill your life. Invite the Holy Spirit to come within. If you encounter any difficulty, put the pen down and ask for help as you look into the flame. Make clear your desire to feel spiritually balanced and ready to fulfill your karmic quest.

24. After you have finished writing, fold the paper in half twice and place it before the lighted candle saying:
"Heavenly Father, I have tried to enter the depths of my own being. I have searched for inner peace and wisdom. Help me to be strong, courageous and willing to bring my body, mind and soul into Thy light. I now look into the divine flame and know my soul is renewed. Amen."

25. Stand by the table and say:
"I ask for clarity and vision to see what I must do. I ask sincerely for help and strength. As I come into the Universal Light I ask a blessing for all those in need and all those I love. Amen."

26. Lighting the seventh candle (behind it is the VIOLET candle), say:
"I recognize the power of God. I light this pure white candle in honor and in love. I ask that I may be blessed and given the power to go within my own soul. I need to discover my purpose and look at my life. I want to examine my relationships so that I can do them all justice. Help me, dear Father, to seek the wisdom of my soul—to know my spiritual path and to follow it in joy. Open up the dark corners of my mind and release Thy heavenly light on all these things. I yearn for Thy nearness and comfort. I open my heart to Thy glory and I will pursue my need for the wisdom within my soul. Help me to appreciate simple joys, to look for you in everything I do from this day on. Amen."

27. Sit again and write clearly your deepest desires. Write what is missing in your life and why. Give thanks for all the many blessings that you have. Stretch your imagination and write

about the things you would like to do. Write about the things you have not done. Open your heart and release all fear and doubt. As you do, be aware that you do all this in the divine light of God the Father.

28. Now you are ready to fold the paper in half twice. Place it before the lighted candle, saying:
"Let me touch into the Light so I may see the many things I must do. Let me do these things in wisdom. I leave behind fear, anger, hurt and all those things that have kept me from the holy Light of God. I am now ready, I am anxious and willing to complete my life journey. I feel my body, mind and spirit is now becoming stabilized in Thy everlasting glory. I am renewed, I am capable of using all the blessings I have received. I protect myself at all times in the glory, wisdom and love of God. Amen."

29. Standing again, now say:
"I now have clarity and vision to see what I must do. I have within me the help and strength that I need. I will remain in the Universal Light and from this Light I ask a blessing on all those in need and all those I love. Amen."

30. Bring your left hand gently over the tips of the seven flames, from candle one through candle seven. Do the same with your right hand from candle one through candle seven, and say:
"I AM SPIRITUALLY RENEWED. I AM IN MY OWN CENTER. STRENGTH IS RISING WITHIN ME. I AM NO LONGER AFRAID. I LOOK FORWARD WITH JOY AND ANTICIPATION TO FULFILLING ALL MY NEEDS IN THE LIGHT OF GOD. AMEN."

Keep the seven WHITE candles lighted for seven minutes and during this time, ask that all of your prayers be granted. Ask for courage and strength to sustain your new spiritual goals. Watch the flames on each of the seven candles and visualize your prayer manifesting, bringing you joy, happiness, success and satisfaction.

Continue to keep the seven candles lighted, and drink from the glass of water on your left. Place it back on the table and drink from

the glass of water on your right, saying:
"I drink this water to cleanse and purify my intent. Amen."

EXERCISE 18: SOLIDIFICATION

In this exercise you will be adjusting the Frequency Structure. You will learn how to allow balancing forces to stabilize your spiritual equilibrium.

You will become more familiar with and sensitive to the intricate vibratory patterns of color: recognizing too much or too little of any one color; being alert to the subtle hues and changes within a color; learning how to interpret the complex vibratory activity that surrounds you at all times. If you have difficulty going to sleep you can discover why. You will enjoy finding out why you react in certain ways—because of too much or too little exposure to particular colors.

There are many ways to test your reactions and also those of family members. Towels, sheets, shirts and bedroom colors all contribute their own energy patterns. (A basic Gnothology chart can provide an immediate complementary color scheme. This works especially well with babies and young children. See *Connolly Book of Numbers*, vols. 1 and 2.) You will find many interesting aspects you can try. Experiment with color but, more importantly, determine what is good for you and why.

Be sure to complete the prior exercise before you begin this one. Note—you may take a small break at this point. Keep the seven WHITE candles burning during this break.

During the process of the last exercise, you determined the influence or level of each number and its corresponding color. When you work with this exercise and you are asked to feel the energy level of each color, you can respond as a result of sensitivity received in the prior exercise. It is from that source that you approach each of the colored candles.

If, in the last exercise, you felt too little of a particular color or a lack of energy associated with the color, you would now focus on the candle in question, and experience the true balance of its color rays. If in the prior exercise you felt too much energy with a color, then in exercise eighteen you would also focus on the candle in question, to bring balance.

The varying shades of any one color denote an increase or decrease of a particular vibratory level. The purpose of this exercise is to adjust to the true color, to correct any imbalance in the vibratory structure. For example, with the RED candle you are dealing with your individuality. Any tendency to be overly aggressive would make you inclined to feel the darker tones of Red. Likewise, if you feel inadequate, or if your self-expression is repressed, you would be inclined to sense a paler Red.

For this exercise you will need an extra WHITE candle. After the candles have been allowed to burn for seven minutes in the prior exercise, light the extra WHITE candle and place it to the far left of your candle grouping.

Before you now, is your original grouping of seven WHITE lighted candles. To the left of this grouping you have an additional WHITE candle, which you light when you are ready to begin this exercise. The additional candle is called the Daath candle.

1. Bring the additional Daath candle from the far left of your grouping, and hold it before you in the center of your body, saying:
   "I recognize the power of God. I am now adjusting my Spiritual Balance in order to avail myself of the correct vibratory flow."

2. Lifting the candle, say:
   "I now raise my Consciousness. Within my flame I bring the Universal Power to all that I am—to all things in my life."

   Now replace the candle to the left of your grouping.

3. Bring the RED candle to the center of the table. As you light the RED candle from the WHITE Daath candle on your left, say:
   "The flame from this candle represents my TRUE INDIVIDUALITY. It is the gift given to me for this life. It is in unison with the heavenly forces. With the power of God I will move within

myself to erase any negativity, reluctance or unwillingness to use this gift correctly."

4. Now place the WHITE Daath candle to the left of the RED candle. Then bring the first of the seven WHITE candles and place it to the right of the RED candle.

   Note—the actual balancing process is from the left and right of any centered colored candle.

   LEFT represents the Daath—the hidden, the source of renewal; the heavenly vibratory forces of pure God energy.

   RIGHT represents how *you* manifest this energy through the color Frequency Structure. Each candle represents the nature of the energy used or misused.

   CENTER represents the type or nature of energy that is now in the process of balance.

   If you feel imbalance on any of the colored candles, it would be corrected in this way: TOO LITTLE requires working from the LEFT to the center. TOO MUCH requires working from the RIGHT to the center.

5. With your arms out toward the left and right candles, become aware of your spiritual balance, in the center. Focus your attention on the RED candle and your TRUE INDIVIDUALITY.

6. As you focus into the center colored candle become aware of any excessive or deficient RED energy. Allow your physical body to be governed by the vibratory flow.

7. Permit your Conscious level to assess the use or non-use of the RED vibration of Individuality. Concentrating on the flame of the RED candle, consciously evaluate how, in fact, you truly and naturally respond to your Individuality.

8. After a full and honest evaluation, close your eyes and allow your physical body to open fully to the flow of Individuality. Be aware of the physical inclination to lean toward one side or the other.

9. When you feel your body swaying to one side, use the other hand to physically pull the hand slowly and deliberately to the

center candle. When you have done this, slowly bring the opposite arm to the center also, thus establishing the perfect and necessary balance required for the particular color vibration you are working with.

10. Still working with your sensitivity, if you need *more* of the energy take your left arm to the left Daath candle and slowly bring the energy toward the center. If you feel that there is still too much emphasis on the right, take your right arm to the candle on the right and slowly, deliberately pull it back to the center colored candle of balance.

   Continue in this way until you have achieved a perfect spiritual balance of the Color Frequency.

11. Feeling in perfect spiritual alignment, reach out and pick up the left and right candles at the same time. Holding them up, say: "I am attuned to the Universal Forces. I am in perfect esoteric balance. I will use this energy in a good and productive way."

12. Replace the candles and looking directly at the flame of the colored candle, inhale a deep breath (feel the intake of energy go through every cell). With the releasing energy, blow out the candle, saying:
   "Thank you, Father, I am now in control. Amen."

13. Repeat this exercise from the beginning with all seven candle colors. Use these areas of focus, and, if possible, add some of your own:

RED	Focus on TRUE INDIVIDUALITY.
	Focus on TRUE STRENGTH.
	Focus on TRUE NEEDS.
	Focus on TRUE DESIRES.
ORANGE	Focus on TRUE COOPERATION.
	Focus on TRUE RELATIONSHIPS.
	Focus on TRUE CONSIDERATION.
	Focus on TRUE CONCERN FOR OTHERS.
YELLOW	Focus on TRUE CREATIVITY.
	Focus on TRUE ENTHUSIASM.

Focus on TRUE EXPRESSION.
Focus on TRUE TALENTS.

GREEN   Focus on TRUE DISCIPLINE.
Focus on TRUE ORGANIZATION.
Focus on TRUE FOUNDATIONS.
Focus on TRUE EFFORT.

BLUE   Focus on TRUE FREEDOM.
Focus on TRUE NEEDS.
Focus on TRUE RESOURCES.
Focus on TRUE VERSATILITY.

INDIGO   Focus on TRUE BALANCE.
Focus on TRUE SERVICE.
Focus on TRUE CONSCIENCE.
Focus on TRUE PURPOSE.

PURPLE   Focus on TRUE WISDOM.
Focus on TRUE INTELLECT.
Focus on TRUE PHILOSOPHY.
Focus on TRUE INSPIRATION.

14. At the completion of *all* seven colors, extinguish each candle, saying:
"I will keep the flame of (name the color of the candle) within myself and use it well. Amen."

CHAPTER SEVENTEEN

THE CLOSENESS OF UNDERSTANDING

Somebody's North is someone else's South. If we travel to the East, we will inevitably arrive in the "West." There are no barriers or obstacles to understanding. For eventually all of us learn from each other and merge. It is in the merging that we see the influences of others.

Man adapts to a continuous flow of knowledge. He chooses immediately whether or not he wants to remember what he has learned. In his attempt to discard, the piece of information is actually recorded in his subconscious. Once something is created within the universe, it remains as part of the universal record or as a part of man's karmic record.

There is no force that can eliminate what has taken place. It is forever recorded in the ether. When man leaves this earth, he also leaves a legacy. The energy he used to retrieve knowledge, knowingly or unknowingly, is still in the ether. Consequently, at some other time, some other place, another mind that is able to tune into the identical retaining level of the original concept can and does, in fact, receive the same information. All it takes is the capacity of another mind to penetrate that particular intelligence. If the intellect of the person receiving the information is competent enough to improve or expand upon it, we see evidence of thrusting beyond the original seed of thought. Around us at all times exists knowledge from all ages. If we are attuned to that thought frequency, we can avail ourselves of this information.

Knowledge never disappears. Knowledge is not just a piece of information—it is embodied in esoteric cells of Light that keep it in the atmosphere. A seeking mind can often touch into these Light cells and receive knowledge hitherto unknown to it. The intelligence of the recipient determines if or how this information will be used.

Children can easily tune in to these esoteric Light cells. Because of inexperience, the child cannot always express what he receives. If the child is outgoing, he will seemingly ask amazing questions and make unusually intelligent remarks. Unfortunately, adults pay little attention to these types of comments.

We should always listen to children! For what is considered "beyond" is often attainable through children and sensitive adults. If we consider the "beyond" as the North, then the bridge of understanding to the South is always there. For example, a person who is spiritually balanced may experience exposure to the esoteric Light cells and retain memory of information received. The knowledge will be filtered through the Consciousness and appear to be magnificent ideas!

Wisdom and knowledge exist on many planes. The diligent student learns how to approach and penetrate these planes of Universal understanding. Before entering this life, the soul is exposed to the Universal levels and knows exactly how to gain access after entering the body. As in a computer, the information is there. All forms of meditation are conducive to accessing the Universal Force. The limited vision of man can be immediately extended once he lifts to the Higher levels.

The Closeness of Understanding is recognizing the possibility. The Cabala contains the esoteric structure we know as the "Tree of Life." Macrocosmically, this Tree represents the structure of the Universe. Microcosmically, it represents the inner structure of man. Here we can see how man is a miniature of the Universe, which explains the saying "As above, so below."

To reach this perfect status, imagine living just *one* day in total balance and perfection—responding on a spiritual level to everything you hear, see, taste, smell and touch. Every minute and every hour of that day, you would be fully aware of your spirituality and relationship with God. You would relate to everything as pure and unblemished.

Before the day was through, every part of the physical body would be inundated with spiritual Light cells. This would remove any obstructive negativity and your spiritual vision would be magnified, giving you a clear view of your true karmic path.

The Closeness of Understanding occurs when man sees what *is*—instead of what he thinks or desires. Understanding your inner purpose and recognizing your link with other souls can open your life in every way. The past and present become one the moment you look to the future. Moving beyond difficulties and self-made obstacles, the soul connects and experiences the Closeness of Understanding.

THE TRUE SELF AND THE EGO

The True Self is the God Self or divine essence of your being. It is the Higher Self, which contains all that is pure, and it is the indescribable link that joins man forever with God and the Universal plan. Man is a unique composition of predestined energies and material elements. The result of this Universal combination is the "True Self."

The ego is a separate substance. Man is like a spider, weaving skillfully to protect himself and bring to him what he needs to exist. It is imperative that man and his ego establish an understanding, otherwise they may oppose each other. This would create a resisting force, abrasive to the desire and intent of the man, or the ego.

When we consider how the ego works, how it supports inner needs and desires, we can see why we would be reluctant to reduce its power. But when the ego is not controlled, it can have a negative effect. The danger is in "becoming" the ego, and forgetting Self. Losing sight of the True Self has its own sequence of events! We lose sight of our karmic path and deny ourselves the soul satisfaction of pursuing our destiny.

The ego is considered to be the individual self—conscious of its separate existence from other selves and things external to itself; capable of thought and feeling usually associated with self-esteem.

Ego is a Latin word that means "I." In mystical or esoteric philosophy, the ego protects and masks the real "I," which is the True Self. The True Self is the "I AM." The ego reflects on the True Self, and becomes the "I AM I."

As children develop, they quickly learn to build the ego. It is used in communicating with parents, teachers and peers. Even at an early age, the child knows how to adjust the ego according to the situation. Parents, for example, are allowed to see more of the "True Self." But as the child learns to play, he extends his ego in other areas. At school he can present an entirely different aspect of his personality. He learns to cover up some of his true personal feelings, and adjusts to the discipline required in his education.

Whether or not the character change is complementary is not the issue. The ego energy weaves a pattern according to the circumstances and the vulnerability of the "True Self." The "True Self" does not always approve of the results!

Having an indirect effect by reflecting itself back upon itself, the ego recognizes its existence as being entirely separate from that which it is. It is like looking into a mirror with another mirror behind you. In esoteric terms, ego is Consciousness that reflects upon itself and in doing so, recognizes its own illusory separateness or existence.

The ego dares to reach out and become involved in the activities of the Conscious mind. As it protects the self, it also creates an expression of personality that is formed as a result of Conscious experience. Fortunately, it can change its nature according to the circumstance. It is adaptable and fragile, for it can be affected or devastated if emotionally challenged. It can be introvert and extrovert as it shapes itself to protect the True Self.

You should always be aware of the ego. In its effort to present its strength, it can base its actions on false foundations. When this occurs, the Conscious mind can be distraught and suffer with emotional impact. Understanding the motivation or spiritual purpose of the True Self requires being aware of the ego. If you know exactly what the ego is trying to express, then the True Self can allow the ego to project its strength under acceptable circumstances. When the ego is out of control, it can do more harm than good.

Your True Self is closely associated with your original karmic intent. It is spiritually motivated to fulfill the requirements of your soul. As you walk upon your life path, your ego protects and expresses this purpose in an outward, worldly way. If it suffers disappointment, it feels bruised but will eventually regain its status.

When the ego is used correctly and intelligently, it can enhance and enlarge the vision of life. If you know and respect its limitations, the ego can boost your personality and encourage personal expression. It is the control of the ego that determines its effectiveness.

The ego can and does bring out inherent talent. The workings of the ego can be rewarding if the ego itself is not permitted full control! As long as the motivation for ego expression is from the True Self, then the manner of the ego would be complementary.

Inner control of the True Self monitors the ego. Consider the True Self as the parent and the ego as the child. It is beautiful to see a child express itself. The spontaneity is delightful and as the child develops, the parent is proud of the results. True Self and ego work in much the same way. An uncontrolled ego can run rampant and cause quite a disturbance in every aspect of life. The True Self must govern the expression of the ego. Then you will experience a well-balanced personality, able to cope with the demands of life on a spiritual and physical basis.

Often we can be misled by the strength of the ego. If we let the ego take over, we can lose sight of who we really are. Insecurity, fear and ignorance can encourage the growth of a false ego. When the ego is morally and spiritually controlled by the True Self, we may see an excellent example of character. Under these conditions, the True Self enjoys the outward expression of ego.

KNOWING IS POWER

Belief in itself is not a passport to knowledge. Believing that all things are possible does open the mind to all possibilities. Unless there is a measure of openness, the mind refuses to accept anything beyond the norm. The field of Esoterics is a vast field of study. It encompasses many areas of undefined spiritual potential.

Our existence is narrowed if we refuse to accept or believe the vastness of the Universe. Since the first evidence of man on earth, we find that in all nations and cultures there has been a positive and repeated urge to discover and explore beyond our normal concepts.

Consider what this world would be like if it were devoid of religion or faith in the unknown. We would live in a world of restricted "show-

and-tell." Imagine further if man were punished or penalized for instigating situations that were not already based on the known! This incredibly narrowed thinking would restrict man so much so that he would be afraid of his own thoughts. Through the centuries, history has recorded the devastation and destruction of human beings that was caused by oppression. In successful attempts to squash man's spirit, everything that represented civilization was destroyed also. This breaking down of social status appears to be connected to man's spiritual, mental and physical growth. If man is robbed of his personal belief system, he then becomes nothing at all. The power of the Universe remains the same and can continue to influence man in all things. It is this power that allows man to rebuild his inspiration, his thirst for knowledge and to establish a personal and satisfying belief system. It is this same power that has filled the minds of men and elevated them to levels of unexplainable attainment.

Imagine if you will, a source of knowledge surging constantly through the Universal Force. Simply by exploring the ways and means to penetrate this vibratory energy, you can gain access. Man is only limited by his belief system. Just recognizing its existence is the key to achieving access. Opening the mind to all possibility expands all the levels of Consciousness. To avail yourself of this magnificent energy, let your mind be open. Be conscious of your spiritual balance and equilibrium. Focus and concentrate via meditation and prayer. Look beyond your present limitations and know that all these things are available to you. This is not merely a promise, this is a fact. When you genuinely accept the existence of a power beyond your own, you then create what you need in the Universe. You enter the Light of the Universe, where all is possible.

THE PERSONAL SEARCH

How did you begin your personal search? What caused your initial interest in the world of parapsychology? Did something unaccountable take place? Or did you meet someone who appeared excited and involved with these mysterious things? Perhaps you read a book or heard a lecture—whatever it was, is absolutely important. Important to you that is—it was the beginning of your personal search.

Your attraction to the extended Consciousness of possibility would indicate that the Higher Self recognized an opportunity. No matter how vague or indifferent the situation, it was sufficient to propel your mind into esoteric regions. Remember, everyone has the potential to discover his own esoteric ability.

The "I AM" is a part of that search. Requiring a sturdy foundation, the "I AM" encourages the "I AM I" to search and provide spiritual nourishment. The reason is that all the unknown exists in spiritual regions. From a simple Divination process, to the skill of a competent parapsychologist—the basic rudiments are the same.

The realms of spirituality consist of many heavenly planes. Within these spheres is the knowledge and wisdom of all time. To penetrate these levels you must basically be rooted, and able to maintain your balance here on earth. Learning how is like learning anything else. The requirements are not only similar but necessary. Learning anything necessitates beginning at the beginning. So the seeking soul must be prepared to do this.

You could appear to be somewhat successful if you experiment and prove particular theories. But becoming truly knowledgeable requires something more than that—a way of life, if you will. A way of thinking and doing things is an essential part of esoteric development. Inevitably, you will reach a level where your spiritual values will be tested.

It is really a simple process of deliberately making effort to retain your spiritual equilibrium. Regardless of emotions and situations, when you are called to the test, the power of spirituality governs and decides all. No one is limited. Educational background cannot provide the esoteric ingredient of spirituality. You can only go so far before you experience resistance or opposition to your purpose. If the soul genuinely wishes to evolve, it is given every opportunity. Keeping this thought in mind enables you to go ahead in confidence.

KNOWLEDGE BRINGS CONFIDENCE

"Jack of all trades, master of none."

There are many misguided souls who eventually fall into Jack's dilemma. If you consider esoteric and spiritual development a necessary part of your life, then it follows that the approach is vital. To learn anything, you must take it step-by-step or lesson-by-lesson. People flounder by not finishing things, not completing studies, always being eager to add information to their repertoire. Little bits and pieces of information become a huge scrap heap that Jack trips over!

Taking a serious interest in one particular aspect does not cause a delay in your studies. In fact, it achieves the opposite. For when you research and study one particular subject, you will have something worthwhile to say about it. Not only that, you also enjoy the time and activity associated with your choice of learning.

One thing always leads to another! By applying diligent interest to your choice of subject, you will see how the separate subjects uniquely blend with each other.

This can happen only when you are entrenched in your initial chosen subject. The knowledge you learn gives you the capacity to understand why and how the various aspects of parapsychology merge. When you recognize the connections, you are on your way to true knowledge. It really doesn't matter where you begin!

Take Tarotology, for example, the art of Divination by using Tarot cards. These cards contain esoteric symbolism that enables the Tarotologist to decipher the hidden depths and counsel accordingly. Tarot eventually leads the student to Gnothology, the Esoteric Science of Numbers, which is also associated with astrology. All these divinatory aspects, each separate to itself, are unified on the Tree of Life. Each is balanced from the identical source, each provides wisdom that is contained within the ancient symbolic structure we know as the Cabala.

The esoteric structure of the Cabala is a complete and original body of knowledge. From its powerful form and divine structure, man can study the esoteric nature of the Universal planes and recognize the reflection within himself. As the student progresses with his choice of subject you can see how, unlike Jack, he becomes proficient and is able to use his knowledge with confidence.

PERSONAL FOUNDATIONS

Before you lay foundations it is necessary to dig deep and to dig well. Familiarize yourself with subject matter that holds interest for you. Explore your natural tendencies. Discover what you enjoy and apply your energy in a pertinent direction. It has been said that in the search for knowledge we take a lonely path. This, I think, is only true to a degree. In your quest for knowledge you enjoy the spiritual journey. This may be a lone journey at times, but you do not necessarily "feel alone." There is a marked difference!

In your pursuit, you *must* have time alone—time to meditate and enjoy the journey of the soul, reaching ever upward to the majestic powers of the Universe. Avoid having your emotions be a part of your foundation unless, of course, they are composed of true joy and the anticipation of achievement. It is imperative to lay solid foundations. The digging is a prerequisite and consists of putting aside doubts and fears. Encourage yourself to be consistent and persistent in your endeavors.

Once this is accomplished, you will have no difficulty in knowing the type of foundation you need to pursue your spiritual goals.

Before placing new foundations you should analyze your present life path. Due to karmic influences, we are usually dealing at any given time with some karmic situation, be it good, bad or indifferent. Karmic obligations are never far away. They certainly cannot be ignored, for the soul urge to rectify, improve or solve is always on the Conscious mind.

This necessitates being aware of what is really happening in our life. I saw this beautifully accomplished by a student of mine who devoted a whole day to contemplating his past, present and future. Having prepared for this special day, he dressed loosely and was fully relaxed. He also fasted, which helped him considerably to focus on his purpose. Finishing in the early evening, he celebrated with a handsome meal and was perfectly happy to have arrived at his conclusions. He felt that he knew exactly where to go from that point.

Not everyone wants to fast and devote a complete day, I realize. But you must absolutely consider the past, the present, and the future events likely to happen unless you make a deliberate spiritual effort to change any undesirable circumstances.

KARMIC OBSTACLES

Karmic obstacles are not always seen. They are felt, and seemingly lurk in the depths of the emotional level. This often feels like a sense of urgency, desperation, or depression without apparent cause. It is important to build your foundations from a good positive spiritual balance. Attempting to build on negativity is like building a house on the edge of the ocean. The emotional waves come in with every tide, and you are constantly in a state of stress.

There are many ways to define karmic obstacles (see *Karma Without Stress*). Everyday situations represent a background for karmic stress. Coping with relationships, work and other obligations are the ingredients of karma. Learning to accept and attune oneself to the Higher forces will provide insight and clarity. The word *karma* is often associated in the mind with drama!

Of course, this is not accurate. The ups and downs of life are often the result of carelessness or not being in command. The inability to make decisions is often the consequence of inadequate choices made in the past. Each relationship is governed by the emotions of all the people concerned. Each painful result presents choices. One choice is to continue as is, to continue suffering and acceptance.

There is an amazing urge to accept everything that anyone can impose or inflict. We nurture the emotional level with excuses like, "There was nothing I could do." This "martyr complex" is a combination of self-pity, lack of personal control, and submission.

I realize that this may sound cold and unfeeling. Yet if you discard the old excuses, you are confronted with real choices. We become accustomed to the imposing vibrations of others, and by accepting them, we demonstrate our incapacity for assuming self-control, and granting people *carte blanche* to manipulate our life. Our apparent inability to control what we want makes it seem like we are not opposed to the interference of others.

TAKING CONTROL FOR SUCCESS

First you must determine the measure of self-control you presently apply. For example, you may be in full control as a business executive. At the same time, you may be overly submissive in personal relationships. This could even account for your executive ability in business! The fact that you lack control in certain situations may cause you to overly compensate. In the reverse situation, we might see someone who is unable to express talent or business acumen because of unsatisfactory working conditions. This could create a need for balance, and we might see this person become overly aggressive in personal relationships.

These examples show how easy it is to take certain situations for granted. Just because you do have some control does not mean that all areas of your life are governed by the same measure of discipline. The first area to examine is in the following exercise.

You may be surprised at how much an unrecognized collection of pressures can affect important issues in your life. By recognition and elimination, you will immediately feel a lift of negative energy. Once you see exactly how things are, you can then build new strong foundations that will support all your future needs. This exercise could be considered the "tax form" of esoterics!

Once it is done, completed and out of the way, you can fully expect a "return"—a substantial "return" to compensate for your stress and labor.

EXERCISE 19: GAINING PERSONAL CONTROL

1. Determine what situations govern your life at this time.
2. Decide whether any of these situations are self-imposed obligations.
3. Separate them into personal and business situations.
4. Decide which of these you would like to improve upon.
5. Which of these need balance?
6. Which of these should be eliminated?
7. What must you do to bring all these situations to the level you require?
8. You have only so much energy. Where should you direct it?
9. What things have you neglected because of unnecessary obligations?

10. How exactly are you going to approach and correct these things?

11. When and how will you start?

12. What are your new goals?

13. Six months from now, how will your life be?

14. Keep a log of positive changes. When will you begin this?

15. Every third month, reevaluate, correct and improve your plan.

After you have answered all these questions you are confronted with "choice." To put yourself in this position is spiritually exhilarating. Think well upon your "choice." Disconnnect yourself from anything negative that brought you to this point. Life feels beautiful and tranquil when you actually take a firm grip and feel the ultimate responsibility of your own thoughts, words and actions.

Keep in mind that making choices changes things. You cannot expect the same situations to happen. Even after you have instigated change, your emotional level will still retain a reflection of what was. But eventually it will dissipate and be replaced with future goals and joy. In the transition, there is a point where the opposing energies merge. This will feel like frustration, confusion and lack of clarity. Understand this process and know that when you feel this energy, all is well! During this transition, something wonderful is also taking place. Your plans are beginning to take root. Deep beneath the apparent confusion there is a strong and powerful growth of your new ideals, goals and happiness.

Your karmic path will become smooth. The rocks of depression will be moved away. You will see the growth of your new and exciting plans. You will have time to smell the flowers as they begin to bloom in every aspect and level of your life. From this spiritual standpoint, you will experience your own inner strength. You will learn to weed out any situation that threatens your new level of joy.

The act of putting your life together the way that you want it to be is *not* the difficult part. The difficulty is in the *decision* to do this. Struggling with fears only adds to a painful dilemma. Make a firm decision, and follow through. After you have acted on your decision, you will find a wonderful encouraging energy. This energy is the power of spiritual strength filling every part of your soul. As the negativity leaves, the inner strength comes in with great power, finds its way, and settles into the places where you previously held fear and unhappiness. Suddenly you feel alive again. Insignificant things start to matter again. You wake up every morning concerned only with progress and joy. This is the secret of life!

Grab it with both hands. Refuse to let your Conscious mind spill its apprehension into your future goals. You are important, you have a part to play. Very simply, this is *your* life. The choices are *yours*.

CHAPTER EIGHTEEN

THE PATTERN OF DREAMS

Many books have been written on the subject of dreams. Some have detailed information with symbolic interpretation. Dreams are a fascinating subject and obviously a message is contained within a dream. We know that everyone dreams. The secret is holding on to the dream memory.

It is not difficult for some. These are the prolific dreamers who have amazing recall and can relate every part of a dream in the finest detail. There are those who have little or no recall of dreams. Much research and study has been done to help people retain the memory of dreams. Nothing is more frustrating than to wake up and know full well that you have been involved in a vivid, complex dream, yet you can't remember it!

Pen and paper on the bedside table help considerably. Take the time to write down every detail as soon as you are able to do so. The Conscious mind can swiftly file the dream memory away. Symbolic images are remindful of what has been stored. This is why it is important to write while you still have recall. Sometimes you may have forgotten a dream, then something occurs that causes instant recollection.

The nature and study of dreams is a deep and engrossing subject. There are skilled analysts who specialize in this field. Constant repetition of the same dream, repeated dream sequences, precognitive dreams—

these should be discussed with a professional counselor who can help interpret any important information you may be receiving.

The subject of dreams opens a vista of study. Freud thought of dreams as an expression of hidden desires merging with memories old and new about life situations. Carl Jung suggested that in some dreams we are exposed to the mystic archetypes. These do not come from the personal Conscious level. In this rare dream situation, the dreamer extracts the mystical archetypes from the Collective Unconscious.

Dreams have eluded, fascinated and tantalized human beings throughout the centuries. There are predictive, or prophetic, dreams. Lucid dreams and High dreams. Astral activities within dreams. When the physical body sleeps, the Conscious mind relaxes and the mysterious levels of our being move swiftly in the night to fulfill, solve, release, and explore the wonders of the Universe.

GNOTHOLOGICAL INTERPRETATION OF DREAMS

In this study we will be concentrating specifically on dream interpretation that uses a Gnothological method of Divination. This method delves deeply into the subconscious and extracts pieces of information, usually in symbolic form. This information can be any part of actual past experience. It can be unfinished business or repressed creativity. It can be bits of emotional memory that time has not been able to dissolve. It can be a collection of fears or hope that has been forced to relinquish its hold because of obligations you were unable to control. Deep in the subconscious are many shapes and forms representing the part of you that has not been fulfilled, a part of you that is still child. Most importantly, this is a part of you that has access to the Higher Consciousness.

The Higher Consciousness is pure Light. When the two levels merge, the subconsciousness is full of Light and reaches to the Higher Consciousness for renewed inspiration and karmic fulfillment. The Higher Consciousness absorbs these messages and gives Light to the symbolic forms absorbed by the subconscious. It does not change these forms—it adds Light only. If the symbolism were changed, the Conscious level would have difficulty understanding.

These symbols are given Light cells by the Higher Consciousness. Through these Light cells the subconscious can recognize what is hidden from the Conscious mind. The Higher Self puts energy into the recorded memories, bringing out visual images. These images are tools to reenact and bring to life seeds of possibility that the Conscious mind can use to begin anew.

As the Higher Consciousness merges with the subconscious, it leaves a residue of karmic memory. This reviving and energizing force influences the Conscious mind so it can receive motivation from karmic experience. The merging of these Conscious levels also produces dreams. The message of a dream can be sometimes very obvious. At other times, the symbology is almost impossible to interpret. Fearful images are sometimes brought to the Conscious mind so you can recognize situations exactly as they are, not as you feared. Symbols can push the Conscious mind forward, showing various karmic abilities, to inspire and create Light on the karmic path.

Look, then, to your dreams. Esoterically, you can make them come true. Once a negative image has been extracted from the subconscious and recognized by the Conscious level, *it is gone*.

DREAMS AND KARMA

Everyday situations and everyday stress is registered in the subconscious. Stress has a way of paralyzing unexpressed karmic needs. Dream images and symbols draw on actors and actresses to perform a play—a story, if you will, that describes with great karmic undertones what is happening emotionally, physically, mentally and spiritually at this time in your life.

Why are dreams usually so unrealistic? The answer is related to the Emotional level. If dreams were totally realistic, life as we know it would not be. Each night we would sleep and live in a realistic reflection of what is. This, of course, would add, rather than avoid, emotional stress. Just imagine having had a bad day, you need some sleep, and presto! The horrendous day is presented all over again.

Likewise, with predictive dreams. Life would be too easy if we were constantly monitored on a nightly basis and informed of tomorrow's activities. This would mean that free will, personal endeavor and karmic responsibility would not exist as such. So all in all, the way we dream is as it should be.

The barrier to understanding dreams is the way we interpret the mystical and sometimes vague images and symbols. By using the Inner Key we can gain insight into our present life situation and recognize the karmic undertones the dream is projecting.

THE INVERTED TRIADIC FORMULA

The origin of this numerical method is ancient, and used in formulating detailed Divination procedures. We use the Inverted Triadic Formula to analyze the source of any dream sequence. The following Letter-to-Number Conversion Table is where we begin the process of finding the DREAM SYMBOL's Inner Key, which is coded "IK."*

Conversion Table

1	2	3	4	5	6	7	8	9
A	B	C	D	E	F	G	H	I
J	K	L	M	N	O	P	Q	R
S	T	U	V	W	X	Y	Z	

The Inverted Triadic Formula is used with a word describing the dream symbol. Within this word there are many answers for decoding the dream sequence. Using the Inner Key method of dream analysis, we will actually probe the suppressed karmic needs.

Using the Inverted Triadic Formula, we evaluate the word *dream* as follows:

---

*The Inverted Triadic Formula is the same formula used to find the Personal Root Number, as described in *The Connolly Book of Numbers*, Vol. II.

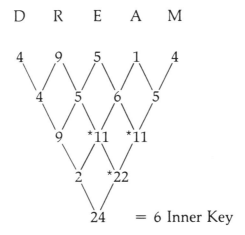

We "reduce" each pair of numbers by adding them, then adding the digits, until we reach a single digit. But there are three Earth Master Vibrations that must *not* be reduced when locating the Inner Key. They are *11, *22 and *33. For example, in the numbers (extracted from the Conversion Table) for the word *dream*, we have an Inner Key total of 24, from the addition of 2+*22=24=6 Inner Key. Note that we do not reduce the *22 to 4. All number totals are reduced *except* these Earth Master Numbers of *11, *22 and *33. Each of the Master Numbers has its own significant interpretation.

How to Compute the Inner Key

1. Using the Conversion Table, we write the symbolic name and place under each letter the corresponding number.

2. For the word *dream*, the first line of numbers is:
   D=4 R=9 E=5 A=1
   M=4   4   9   5   1   4

3. The second line of numbers:
   4+9=13=4 9+5=14=5 5+1=6
   1+4=5   4   5   6   5

4. The third line of numbers:
   4+5=9 5+6=*11 6+5=*11   9   *11   *11

5. The fourth line of numbers:

$9 + {}^*11 = 20 = 2$ ${}^*11 + {}^*11 = {}^*22$ 2 ^{*22}

6. The fifth line of numbers:

$2 + {}^*22 = 24 = 6$ 6   Inner Key

7. When the inverted triad reaches a single digit, or is reduced to an Earthly Master Number (EMV), we then have the Inner Key.

USING THE INNER KEY

The Inner Key is the number derived (by the Inverted Triadic Formula) from the symbol your Conscious mind remembers about your dream.

For example, Mary remembers dreaming about eating cherries. Over and over, she tries to remember more about the dream. Eventually she talks about it with her friend and remembers that in another part of the dream, she was sewing a new dress.

May could analyze her dream by focusing on these two issues: eating cherries, and sewing a new dress.

To do this, we use only the words *cherries* and *sewing*. The Inner Key should be derived from just *one* word, the main symbol from your dream.

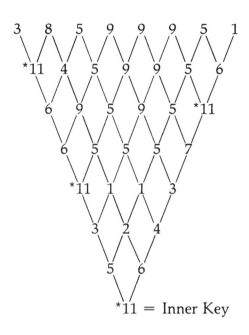

C H E R R I E S

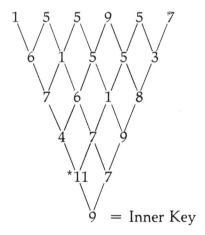

S E W I N G

Dream symbols:	Cherries	Sewing
Inner Keys:	= *11	= 9

From the Inner Key we receive karmic insight. Using the Inner Key takes us to the basis of the dream, the KEY WORD.

From a Cabalistic point of view, using the Inner Key takes us directly to the karmic source. What part of our esoteric being needs to be expressed, and why? Adjusting to the message of the Inner Key will immediately improve life and circumstances on the Conscious level. It will eliminate the need for further stress. The Inner Key provides the fruit on the Tree of Life.

Here are the Key Words, the "messages" of the dream, for each Inner Key:

Index of Inner Keys

INNER KEY	KEY WORD
1	INDIVIDUALITY
2	COOPERATION
3	CREATIVITY
4	DISCIPLINE
5	FREEDOM
6	BALANCE
7	WISDOM
8	POWER
9	RELEASE
*11	VISION
*22	CONTROL
*33	SUCCESS

The Last Triad

The last three numbers of the Inverted Triadic Formula are an important part of the interpretation of the Key Word. After finding the actual Inner Key, the last of the three numbers—known as the Last Triad, we use the next to last two numbers (called the "Root Direction") to analyze the root of the Inner Key.

So, from the Last Triad, we use the first two numbers for the Root Direction. This gives you more information about the Inner Key.

For the word *cherries*:

Last Triad	= 5	6 *11
Root Direction	= 5	6
Inner Key	= *11	(the last number in the Last Triad)

The 5 and 6 are used to analyze the Inner Key of *11. The 5 and 6 are the Root Direction.

Through the *11, which is the Inner Key, Mary is being told to look toward a new future vision. In fact, the dreamer is being clearly told she can expect to receive clarity about future happenings. The Root Direction, 5 followed by 6, shows the initial steps that must be taken.

Mary should become resourceful, more flexible and use versatility in present conditions. She should learn how to balance present obligations, relationships and all other activities. Then she can look forward to receiving with great clarity the future vision for expanding her present life-style.

For the word *sewing*:

Last Triad	= *11 7 9
Root Direction	= *11 7
Inner Key	= 9

Sewing was also part of Mary's dream. The Master *11 is emphasized. The first part of the dream that Mary remembered was the Cherries, and that Inner Key was also *11.

The two Inner Keys are two stages that Mary must go through. We begin with the second Inner Key of *11, which Mary can achieve through the analysis and application of 5 and 6. Then we come to a second level of Root Direction, *11 and 7, to achieve the Inner Key of 9.

Concentrating on the Master *11, Mary must in the second stage concentrate on her Inner Wisdom. She must think deeply and learn to rely on her intuition. She must not lose sight of her future visions and plans. Allowing a natural flow of inherent karmic abilities to surface, her karmic strength is going to manifest. Past talents will become part of her new vision. Although seemingly new, she will, in fact, be using talents that have been perfected in a previous lifetime.

Once Mary puts faith in herself, she will gain the power she needs to extricate herself from unwanted situations. So faith in her own ability is what she must act upon at this time. As you can see, the Inner Keys open the mystical gates of the Consciousness. Through what might have been an undetectable message from the depths of Mary's Consciousness, we see a vital karmic message in the simple symbols of Cherries and Sewing.

There are some people who remember dreams of long ago, often vivid, simple situations. If you have a memory of a dream, you can still discover the message of the Inner Key. It is interesting to record the date of your dreams for future reference.

Triple Triad

When numbers are repeated it very definitely puts emphasis on that particular numerical energy force. If, for example, you encounter a Triple Triad, then the dream sequence has revealed powerful karmic energy that stimulates all levels of Consciousness.

A Triple Triad occurs when the resulting Inner Key number is repeated elsewhere in the delineation another three times. That means that the number is located a minimum of three times in the delineation *plus* it is also the final Inner Key number.

In the example of Cherries is a Triple Triad of *11. In the example of Sewing, there is no Triple Triad.

In analyzing Mary's dream further, we can see that through the two dream symbols, the need to understand the Master *11 must occur before she experiences the Inner Key of 9.

The power of the Inner Keys can be used daily. Dreams emphasize a need, and the Inner Keys give you immediate insight for the part of your life that is experiencing stress.

DAILY USE OF INNER KEYS

Reference to the Inner Keys on a regular basis can help you express your hidden needs without trauma or fear. Understanding how to adjust your life each day will provide you with a clear vision and outlook.

Using the Inner Keys daily helps you recognize your strengths and weaknesses. On a day-to-day basis, the whole process is simplified. Difficulty and stress arise when we permit others to control and direct. Consistent self-monitoring will eliminate daily stress. You may also have hidden pressures! Long-standing pressures are not always easy to find. They can easily become part of your personality. Because of their longevity, it is possible that you are not aware they exist.

The secret is—if you don't feel right, then something is wrong. Use the Inner Keys to discover why.

Remember! With every level of expression, there is a positive and a negative aspect. The Point of Balance should be the constant goal.

UNDERSTANDING YOUR DREAM

Everyone can interpret their dreams using the esoteric Inner Keys. Whatever you remember is sufficient to receive the message from your Higher Self. This makes dreaming an adventure and a source of knowledge for everyone. Just one word, and you can receive information you can use immediately. You no longer need to struggle to recapture the dream sequence. Only out of personal interest should this be done. From an esoteric point of view, all you have to have is exactly what you remember!

It is important to identify exactly "what you remember." Upon waking, you write down, in the order of memory recall, the first words you think of.

For example, as you recall the dream, if you think of a plane, don't write the word *airplane*, write *plane*. If your first impression of a dream symbol is of gold, don't write *golden*, write *gold*. The first descriptive word that comes into the Consciousness is exactly the word you need to discover the Inner Key. If you remember a boy, write the word *boy*.

If later you remember it was a boy you know, and his name is Alan, then write *Alan* in the order it occurred to you.

The sequence of the Inner Keys is vital to correct interpretation. Afterthoughts do not take priority on your list of symbols. They are important additions to the message of the Inner Keys.

SAMPLE DREAM ANALYSIS

Here is a sample dream, one that my son Peter had:

1. He saw his sister Louise: LOUISE
2. He saw a plane: PLANE
3. The plane wrecked, and no one was hurt: WRECK
4. He was with his brother Jon: JON
5. They wanted to see Vietnam: VIETNAM
6. He was with his friend Todd: TODD
7. They wanted to see Vietnam: VIETNAM

The seven Dream Symbols are in the order Peter recalled the fragments of his dream. He was aware that more happened, but could not remember what. Taking these seven symbols in the sequence of his recall, we can find the Inner Key for each symbol:

$$L \quad O \quad U \quad I \quad S \quad E$$

$$3 \quad 6 \quad 3 \quad 9 \quad 1 \quad 5$$

$$9 \quad 9 \quad 3 \quad 1 \quad 6$$

$$9 \quad 3 \quad 4 \quad 7$$

$$3 \quad 7 \quad {}^*11$$

$$1 \quad 9$$

$$1 \quad = \text{Inner Key}$$

P   L   A   N   E

7   3   1   5   5

  1   4   6   1

    5   1   7

      6   8

        5   = Inner Key

W   R   E   C   K

5   9   5   3   2

  5   5   8   5

    1   4   4

      5   8

        4   = Inner Key

J   O   N

1   6   5

  7   *11

    9   = Inner Key

V   I   E   T   N   A   M

4   9   5   2   5   1   4

4   5   7   7   6   5

9   3   5   4   *11

3   8   9   6

*11   8   6

1   5

6 = Inner Key

T   O   D   D

2   6   4   4

8   1   8

9   9

9 = Inner Key

Then, using the Index of Inner Keys (above), we can make this chart:

DREAM SYMBOL	INNER KEY	KEY WORD
1. Louise	1	Individuality
2. Plane	5	Freedom
3. Wreck	4	Discipline

4. Jon	9	Release
5. Vietnam	6	Balance
6. Todd	9	Release
7. Vietnam	6	Balance

Peter's Higher Self first refers to his Individuality. At this time in his life he is totally free to express who he is. From this Freedom, he can establish a new Discipline. The dream suggests that there are a couple of things he must release to acquire the inner balance he needs.

Additional note: Peter's Gnothology chart shows that his dream is compatible with his natal structure. These important aspects of the dream are also current aspects in his Gnothology chart.

To remember just one aspect of a dream is very important. The Higher Self is attempting to give you information.

The following Dream Symbols all have Triple Triads.

LOUISE	1	Individuality
PLANE	5	Freedom
VIETNAM	6	Balance
VIETNAM	6	Balance

The Triple Triads indicate strong karmic forces at work. Although LOUISE appeared only briefly in the dream, the symbol is very powerful and indicates that Peter is now at a karmic level where he is to express his true Individuality.

A new kind of Freedom is recognized when it is emphasized with a Triple Triad. This Freedom will come about as Peter Releases his new Individuality. We see that Vietnam is repeated twice, and this gives a Double Triple Triad. If all these karmic changes are taking place, then he will be given all the necessary energy to readjust his Balance. It is from this new Balance that he will project his inherent karmic talents.

WORKING WITH THE INNER KEYS

Life is constantly moving. Sometimes it is fast and furious, other times, calm and satisfying. Sometimes life appears to be at a standstill.

With so many obstacles looming before us, there are times when we feel far behind on our life course. Because of these highs and lows, the Inner Key Code is arranged into separate aspects. Wherever you are on your karmic path you may gain additional help by following that part of the code most suited to your present situation.

These five aspects of life are present within each Inner Key number:

Self

Relationships

Talents

Personal

Business

If you are not sure where your difficulty lies, you may discover its origin by consulting *all* aspects of each Inner Key number. You can also study the Root Directions and Triple Triads, by reading the aspects and considering the findings with a lesser degree of emphasis.

EXERCISE 20: INNER KEY 1—INDIVIDUALITY

INDIVIDUALITY: The condition of having a distinct and separate existence. It is the total sum of your characteristics and personal traits that makes you who you are.

Self

Suppressing your Individuality can cause a lack in many areas of your life. Your Individuality is not a monster to be hidden in the depths of yourself! It is a vital and necessary energy to use along the karmic path. Without the full and easy expression of your own individual personality, you will be open and submissive to the Individuality of others.

Always remember, those who have no problem with self-expression have *learned* to be this way. They have made mistakes and errors before reaching the ability to *be* who they are. Dream images in this group stress the need for you to "blossom," to express that unique inner energy in ways that say, "This is me."

If you do not normally assert your Individuality it might be difficult for you to recognize it exactly! It is that part of you that needs to vocalize and express exactly how you feel. It is that part of you that yearns for the freedom to be who you are. You will never know if you have the potential to be successful unless you have the courage to try anyway. Avoid being intimidated by others. Recognize that there is a part of you that is equal to any other. It is this inner strength that lies sleeping like a lion deep inside, with a continual longing for personal freedom.

SEARCHING FOR AN ANSWER:

1. Release yourself entirely from undesired situations.
2. If this seems difficult, take the time to consider why.
3. Recognize that you are a valuable person.
4. Look at who you are. Examine your needs, and your strengths.
5. Allow all aspects of your personality to surface.
6. Look directly into why you have problems in "being you."
7. Let go of fear, and refuse to feel threatened or intimidated.
8. Be prepared to make adjustments, and don't look back.
9. Be considerate of your own needs. Make new rules.
10. Freedom of the soul is freedom of Individuality.

Relationships

Too much Individuality will domineer and overpower people. Too little will make you submissive. Too much or too little Individuality does not complement any relationship.

Talents

Applying your Individuality to your talents will ensure constant input into the expression of these talents. Applying your Individuality to your talent can help you attain your goals.

Personal

The test of true Individuality is in this category. If you feel content and secure, then your Individuality is in balance. If you are overly subservient and constantly strive to please, then you need to assert yourself to reach the Point of Balance. On the other hand, if you are overly aggressive and constantly strive to prove your point of view, this will alienate you from the very things you seek in life.

Business

Individuality must be used in business affairs. The challenge is to learn how. It has nothing to do with position or prestige. It is a matter of knowing who you are and respecting yourself for the things you do. If you feel non-productive, consider whether you are in the right job. If you are successful, be sure it is a genuine personal success, and not at the expense of others. Individuality at its best is good leadership and accepting your position with pride and accomplishment.

EXERCISE 21: INNER KEY 2—COOPERATION

COOPERATION: The act of cooperating and uniting effort. The joining together or combination of persons for purposes of joint productivity for their joint efforts.

Self

True Cooperation requires the art of giving and receiving equally. In close relationships, this skill must be mastered sufficiently to ensure that the two people concerned create the necessary bond needed to stay together. The closer the relationship, the more this level is tested. Establishing a sensitivity between each other helps determine when to give and when to receive. Learning the art of Cooperation eventually adds strength to each person's capabilities. Having another person who understands your personal efforts, and having the support of this person, does indeed give additional strength to accomplish all you want.

Cooperation is "sharing," receiving the support from another and knowing when to return this support. It is the Point of Balance. Spiritually, the Universe and man exist cooperatively. Experiencing the essence of joy, delighting in someone else receiving as though it were given to you—these are examples of this wonderful energy.

The measure of giving and taking is often out of balance. When we expect with no reason then we expect beyond reason. If you are continually giving, you should examine why. If the answers are good and add to your sense of well-being, then all is well. But if you feel depleted, exhausted and in constant turmoil, you should take action to correct the situation. Be it in personal relationships or business relationships, adjustment is required.

SEARCHING FOR AN ANSWER:

1. Are you giving too much or too little?
2. Do you have difficulty in sharing?
3. Are you lonely and in need of companionship?
4. Are you experiencing stress because of a relationship?
5. What do you expect from this relationship?
6. Is it a constant struggle to maintain relationships?
7. Is it easy and natural to be the "real you"?
8. Do you feel trapped and unable to escape?
9. What changes are you going to make?

Relationships

Your relationships should be complementary to your life goals. Maintaining relationships that have no value and cause consistent stress is destructive. Karmic ties may bind you, but if you consider that you have repaid your karmic obligations it is time to sever these ties and go on your way! Otherwise, you may be accumulating more karma!

Talents

If you truly have a desire to use your talents and you feel that you have a blockage because of another person, then it's a good idea to analyze the situation. A good solid relationship does not give a negative input to your talent—or indeed, to the other person's talent.

Personal

Self-love and self-respect are where you must build from. Without these ingredients you cannot make or develop any successful relationship. *Gnothi Seauton* means *know thyself*. Know what you want, know your needs and aspirations. Develop self-confidence and you will attract exactly what you want—be it a satisfying relationship, an expression of talent or any other aspect of life. Being yourself, and knowing what makes you content and happy, are very important. A relationship can only add to this. A relationship cannot be the entire reason for your contentment and spiritual joy. You must also enjoy and appreciate who *you* are. This makes you better able to find a relationship where you truly complement each other.

Business

Cooperation is the key in any business situation. Incurring difficulty in your work suggests dissatisfaction with the position itself or the colleagues around you. Determine which it is, or if it is both. The deterioration of one will inevitably affect the other. If any part of you is not happy in your working situation, you should investigate why. If it cannot be solved, then you have no alternative but to look elsewhere. After all, if you are not satisfied, then you will not be giving your best and this will only add to the dilemma.

EXERCISE 22: INNER KEY 3—CREATIVITY

CREATIVITY: Having the power to create, to bring into being, to produce from one's own thoughts and imagination. To bring forward ideas and translate them into reality.

Self

We grow and evolve by receiving ideas and working with these ideas to create. Many people have brought karmic talents into this life. The constant urge to create something special is a sure sign of inherent karmic talent. When ideas seemingly pop into your head, they should be given consideration before you forget them. Listen to your inner needs and permit yourself to follow through. However magnificent or humble your talents may be, this is not the issue. Allowing yourself the personal freedom of trial and experiment is vital to your spiritual growth.

Knowing that someone else could do something better is not a reason for not trying. A mother creating a beautiful birthday cake gains a deep sense of satisfaction. Perhaps she is aware that some great pastry chef could do a more artistic job, but her concern is to express her own talents. The rewards are always there, if only in the eyes of her child! What better reward could there be?

Little children enjoy expressing and exploring all possibilities. This joyful gift is *not* taken away. It is always there, ready to be used. Ignoring the inner desire to create can affect many other areas of life. A sense of dissatisfaction can shed gloom over every effort. A man who sits at his desk all day might thoroughly enjoy planting a few flowers. The measure of your Creativity is not important. The *expression* of what you feel is very important. Never ignore the "little one" inside. Feel free to be who you are and you may be amazed when you see the results. A nagging and persistent urge to do something may be the key to opening Pandora's Box. But unless you explore everything that you are, you will never know the joy of Creativity.

SEARCHING FOR AN ANSWER:

1. Do you have a desire to create something?
2. Would you like free time to do something different?
3. Do you think of certain things you would like to do?
4. Have you ever imagined expressing an unusual talent?
5. What kind of things would you like to try?
6. What obstacles have you made to prevent trying?
7. When did you last enjoy using your Creativity?
8. What do you need to start being creative?
9. In what ways do you express your True Self?
10. What secret talent do you think you have deep inside?

Relationships

Creativity in relationships is absolutely necessary. The continual effort to create and develop contributes to the strength of the relationship. Time and circumstance has a way of making us change. Within these changes we must be versatile—not only willing but prepared to create within new conditions. Unfortunately, many relationships have ended simply because at the beginning, the natural urge to express was repressed or denied. Later, when it becomes important to show this side of our self, our partner lacked understanding. We then speak of outgrowing the relationship, or each other.

Talents

Creativity is the energy that channels hidden talents and brings them to the surface. This natural urge should never be suppressed. It should be investigated with care, and encouraged if it withstands the investigation. Often inherent talent remains sleeping if the Higher Self sees that, due to circumstance, the talents would meet frustration. At an opportune time in life, the Higher Self releases the urge. This accounts for talents that surface later in life.

Personal

Personal Creativity tells the world who we are. Grooming, style, and the things that surround us are all part of our personal expression. Society recognizes this and, unfortunately, we are presented with images that are not always the result of true personal Creativity. Too often we look to these outside things for the image we wish to project, rather than creating our own expression. The way you speak and relate to people, the way you project yourself, is all part of personal Creativity.

Business

When it comes to business we find a tremendous outlet for Creativity—if you are in the right business situation. If you feel limited in your expression, then the work that you are doing may not allow you to satisfy your need to be creative. Creativity is not simply being artistic as such. Creativity is expressing yourself through what you do. It is using your own unique way of producing results.

EXERCISE 23: INNER KEY 4—DISCIPLINE

DISCIPLINE: A state of order that maintains training and control. Regulations for conduct and efficiency. The mind or character acting according to rules established.

Self

Rules and regulations are everywhere and in every way of life. Some we readily adhere to, others we resent if we feel they impose on our sense of privacy. The kind of Discipline we are speaking of is "self-discipline." Without it, we have no rules to follow. There are no boundaries, yet a person without self-discipline continually bumps up against the boundaries others have made.

Life itself is Discipline, so if we act in an undisciplined manner, we become out of balance with all that is. To respect Discipline, it must be established within. A disciplined person can understand the disciplines of others. The physical body relies on the Discipline you apply. Too much food and no exercise, and you become overweight.

Too much of anything and life becomes out of balance. The old saying, "All work and no play makes Jack a dull boy" is perfectly true. All aspects of life must be considered. Recreation and work are each necessary. Applying Discipline makes goal achievement much easier. Discipline in all things is an absolute must. Without it we will have chaos and constant upheaval in life.

SEARCHING FOR AN ANSWER:

1. Lack of success indicates lack of foundations.
2. Without Discipline, you have no power to improve.
3. Are you presently trying to accomplish a goal?
4. Have you built firm and solid foundations?
5. Without foundations, the least provocation will destroy your efforts.
6. Ideas can prosper if they are established firmly.
7. Are you careless when it comes to planning?
8. Gaining successful results requires planning.
9. Every time you try, do you fail?
10. Why?

Relationships

No relationship can survive without Discipline—it is destined to end before it really begins. Once the root of Discipline is applied, your efforts will be fruitful. Discipline can seem restricting, *and it is!* Without it, we can rely on nothing. Without order, there is disorder, and we will not derive any love or satisfaction from that level.

Talents

Unless you look closely, talents and Discipline do not seem related. Yet they are. Anything capable of growth requires Discipline, otherwise it is tossed about by the elements. Talent requires the power of Discipline to make it withstand any opposing influences.

Personal

Personal Discipline makes us what we are. It can be detected in our every personal expression. The way we conduct our lives reveals the measure of Discipline we live by. Discipline is *ultimately* freeing. It paves the way for true and sincere expression. It monitors our thinking, and therefore it shows. It is evident in our personality, and if it is lacking, others will be repelled by our lack of self-control and our disorder.

Business

The way you apply Discipline in working conditions will determine the responsibility delegated to you. Don't leave home without it! Promotions and salary increases are all associated with your ability to Discipline yourself and the work you do. Lack of Discipline in the workplace can be disastrous.

EXERCISE 24: INNER KEY 5—FREEDOM

FREEDOM: Liberation from confinement or constraint. Liberty, independence. Ease of movement and free use. Freedom to be you.

Self

Inner personal Freedom is the passport to all other levels. Without inner Freedom, you have no access to the qualities and advantages of other levels. Your inner sense of personal Freedom overcomes all fears. It rapidly takes you away from failure. It allows you to be who you are. There is no substitute for inner personal Freedom. You must have the physical, mental and spiritual space to express everything that you are and can be.

People often disregard or relinquish their inner Freedom at the drop of a hat. The whole concept of Freedom is attached to the meaning of karma—not social standing or unavoidable situations—but the inner Freedom that is a reflection of spirituality. If we lose sight of this inner Light, aspirations and future goals are dimmed by self-imposed restrictions.

To achieve life goals and recognize your karmic path, it is imperative to retain your inner sense of Freedom. We are born with everything we need to accomplish our spiritual goals. No matter how demanding life becomes, we always have access to the inner Light of Freedom. Once you accept the importance of inner Freedom, you will readily see that, regardless of your present situation, you are free to think, change, adapt, improve and reject. With a constant awareness of the inner Light, you are free to use your personal Freedom. Any hindrance in life begins with your own denial of your personal Freedom. Your efforts and goals cannot be rooted firmly and correctly unless you are continually aware of this strength. Personal Freedom is the greatest gift. With this energy, you can be who you are. Always be aware of this gift. Life may be problematic, but as long as the Light of inner Freedom is bright you have access to every part of your being. This Light touches upon every facet of your ability. It can search and probe all levels of Consciousness, and provide whatever is needed to retain its Light. Look into the darkness of your dilemma and you will find this Light. It will swiftly move away from your problem and burn brightly into the area of you that is capable of solving and presenting the required solution.

SEARCHING FOR AN ANSWER:

1. Know that you are totally free to make choices.
2. By making choices you are using the inner Light.

3. The inner Light will show what you need to do.

4. What limitations have you imposed on yourself?

5. In what areas do you need to make choices?

6. With the inner Light you *can* see beyond your limitations.

7. What prevents you from being free?

8. When are you going to act on these things?

9. Fear of fear is completely devastating.

10. Get in command of yourself *now*. This is Freedom.

Relationships

Having a close relationship does not mean giving up inner personal Freedom. A good strong relationship is enhanced by the *two* inner Lights of you and your partner, each expanding radiantly as they reflect on each other. Being close does not mean that one partner has to extinguish the inner Light of Freedom. A true and meaningful relationship means the opposite—each complementing and contributing to the other.

Talents

It would appear that there is one Universal excuse. That is, "I don't have the time." How often have you said or heard that? It is possible that you believe it! You know, talent is *not* a *hobby*. It is a part of you that yearns to be expressed. The measure of your talent does not matter. The part of you that is creative and rooted in past life experience needs to surface. The sensitivity embraced in your talent is a beautiful aspect of you. If it is not used, then part of you is in limbo. As you begin to express your talents, this unused aspect of your personality emerges to expand all your potential.

Personal

Have the personal Freedom to be who you are in all things. Be unafraid and willing to put this part of yourself in everything you do. The real you is free! Hiding this part of yourself will limit all sources of personal joy and happiness. Feeling fulfilled is the reward of Freedom. It may topple false hopes but it will fortify true goals. Everything you *are* has to be part of everything you *do*.

Business

Freedom gives you choice and experience determines your choice. In business situations the ego must not stand in the way of reality. If you feel competent, then you will feel free to express your skills in business. If you are not competent, then your Freedom is limited. Eliminate barriers by applying your inner Freedom to the right areas. You are free to learn and improve your skills, if necessary. If you are not satisfied with your working situation, or you lack certain requirements, then use your Freedom to improve and progress.

EXERCISE 25: INNER KEY 6—BALANCE

BALANCE: Authoritative control. A state of equilibrium. Composure and stability. Harmony within and without. Spiritually, to balance and be conscientious in all things.

Self

Where there is upset, there is a lack of Balance. The Point of Balance equates the satisfaction in what you do with what you accept from others. The Point of Balance is *you*. It may be difficult to distinguish "satisfaction" from "acceptance," yet there is a vast difference. Satisfaction is achieving your desire, whereas acceptance is settling for whatever happens, whether or not it is what you want. To be satisfied, you must have been committed to reaching a goal. To simply accept suggests that you were willing to settle for less.

Since Balance represents remaining centered, then nothing less can be considered acceptable. It means being yourself. Spiritually, Balance is a natural state of being. That is why the soul craves peace, Balance and harmony. Exposed to life and the complications of karmic endeavor, it is possible to fall away from this Point of Balance. But unlike goals, where we have to stretch and exercise effort, Balance is a natural state of being. Consciously remaining balanced in all things, thoughts, words and deeds will always bring you back to your karmic path.

SEARCHING FOR AN ANSWER:

1. Lack of Balance causes continuous stress.
2. Do you feel stress?
3. What areas of your life are causing you stress?
4. What is required in these areas to establish Balance?
5. Are you willing to analyze and correct?
6. When you feel out of Balance, everything seems difficult.
7. Health problems can arise when you are out of Balance.
8. Make a plan to correct, and a goal to achieve.
9. Are others affected by your lack of Balance?
10. What can you do about it and *when*?

Relationships

Make no mistake, *all* relationships are affected when you are out of Balance. You may think you can hide your true feelings but no matter what the relationship is, everyone is affected. This includes children, loved ones, business colleagues and, more importantly, you yourself. The energies you give to every situation are colored by how you feel.

When you correct your Balance, then your energies are distributed to the areas of concern that have been concentrated in the wrong direction.

Talents

As stress and pressure require additional energy, other areas of your life become neglected. Your talents truly suffer. Balance is essential and if you suffer from lack of Balance, your talents may appear nonexistent. When all focus is channelled to a negative and undesirable energy, the rest of your life is in chaos. Everything is affected when you lose your inner Balance. Talents suffer especially, for there is no joy of expressing the True Self.

Personal

You can never ignore the terrible feeling of depression that comes with lack of Balance. It is a heavy and compelling feeling. It is relentless in its constant urging. All levels of Consciousness seek to find inner Balance. Without it, you cannot see or plan ahead.

Your attention is constantly focused on the negative conditions. Always remember, it can only get worse! It will not disappear in the night—in fact, it becomes more active in the night. Face the cause, confront the cause, eliminate the cause. Unless you do, the Balance will further deteriorate and things will become even worse. Take a deep breath and get in control *now*.

Business

Without Balance, the first signs of danger appear in relating to others at work. Your productivity is also affected, and will continue to be affected, until you have corrected the situation. Mistakes, cover-ups, excuses are all signs to be heeded. Spending eight hours every day in a work situation, being out of Balance, cannot possibly go unseen or unnoticed! Delve into the problem and deal with it. Nothing else will do. You need your precious Balance to conduct your business. The moment you begin to solve your situation, everything will start coming back in place.

EXERCISE 26: INNER KEY 7—WISDOM

WISDOM: The quality of being wise. Sound judgement and the truth to act accordingly. Common sense, knowledge. The faculty to determine right and wrong and apply to self.

Self

Wisdom is like a rough stone given to man. As man develops and learns to live with himself and others, his efforts are known in the heavens. The rough stone is carved through personal experience and is polished by the way man uses his Wisdom. It is seen and respected in Heaven and on earth alike.

The mind of a child often seems more open to Wisdom than that of an adult. The child is eager and seeks new knowledge. This is the way the child grows. Frequently we see the refusal to learn by the adult. Discovering new knowledge requires a childlike curiosity and most adults have far too many problems to explore that concept. Gathering and understanding the knowledge we gain is not sufficient. You acquire Wisdom when you put knowledge to practical use. Knowing is one thing; acting or behaving based on knowledge is another. Wisdom is experience—rounded experience. A wise man never stops searching until he has grasped the complete concept—until he *knows* that he knows. Too often, we have the experience and don't learn anything from it. Experience carves the character. It does not become Wisdom until the images of that experience become part of the whole person.

SEARCHING FOR AN ANSWER:

1. Wisdom is truth learned from experience.
2. Life presents opportunities to learn and acquire Wisdom.
3. Repeated mistakes is the denial of the Higher Self.
4. When faced with a problem, do you take time to think it through?

5. What have you learned from past experience?

6. Inner Wisdom allows the intellect to merge with Spirit.

7. Take the time to stop and think before you respond.

8. What areas of your life continually disturb you?

9. Are you afraid of not getting what you want?

10. Do you act irresponsibly and regret it afterwards?

Relationships

Using knowledge gained from past relationships can help you avoid repeating the same errors. If one important relationship failed to provide a particular need, think carefully before you hear yourself making that demand from a new relationship. Consider whether you are looking for that missing element or honestly enjoying a new relationship for exactly what it is. In some relationships you will find a stronger bond than in others. Allow your Higher Self to inspire and guide you. You may, for example, have a definite karmic bond between you. In many relationships the karma involved requires both souls to adjust and compensate each other.

Talents

Talents are a result of past life experience! That is why talents should not be ignored. Talents are part of who you are and have been. Man is capable of all things. When he has a need, he uses particular talents in a specific lifetime. As part of man's experience here on earth, he is always born with new potential.

This would account for incomplete expression of an inherent talent. The limitation is not ability but need. The talent will be perfected in a future life experience.

Personal

A sense of personal accomplishment is achieved only when we made an effort. Your personal well-being depends on the inner peace that only such effort brings. Even the knowledge that you tried and failed becomes Wisdom, because the experience is recorded. Therefore you accumulate Wisdom, through the combination of experience and knowledge. The test, of course, is whether or not you avail yourself of this Wisdom. Once gained, it will always remain, until it is used again and increased by further experience.

Business

The use of Wisdom is critical in any work situation. You must retrieve the knowledge stored by personal experience. Unless this is done on a regular basis, you could not hope to keep your position in life. Wisdom covers all areas of expression. The Higher Self is constantly submitting messages. And it is foolish to deliberately cut your self off from this source when you leave work. Yet we see this in many people. Busy, productive people often make stupid errors in private situations. Wisdom is like a huge umbrella. It protects as long as we keep it up.

EXERCISE 27: INNER KEY 8—POWER

POWER: The ability to do or act. A particular faculty of body or mind. Strength, force, energy to exercise authority.

Self

The test of spirituality when we possess Power is how we use it for ourselves and others. Some people are afraid of their own magnitude of Power and are hesitant to use it. Others use it excessively to manipulate and establish their needs. When our own Power is obviously misused, we can find the cause. All we have to do is recognize that the act of Power had its origins in a past experience that has not yet been transformed into Wisdom.

Exercising Power with such recognition will ultimately erase the original experience. This will be noticeable in future acts or attempted demonstrations of this Power.

If we look into history, we can see how powerful human beings destroyed their own Power. We call this "self-destruction." Self-destruction occurs when we do not allow the Higher Self to transform experience into Wisdom. The Power becomes inverted, causing destruction.

The word *Power* suggests strong, firm actions. This is true, but we must also consider other expressions of Power, which can be equally effective. Gentleness and compassion are ways to express and expand upon Power.

These qualities are quickly absorbed into Wisdom, and the Power continues to grow when it is exposed to the spiritual input of the Higher Self. Before we can fully appreciate the quality of Wisdom we must know how it thrives and multiplies. Wisdom is spiritual and it adheres itself to the soul. Before it can manifest outwardly, it must replenish itself inwardly.

SEARCHING FOR AN ANSWER:

1. Has your life experience been transformed into Wisdom?
2. Think well on the Power you now have.
3. Looking back on life, can you see if you lost any Power?
4. If so, can you see why?
5. How can you best use your Power?
6. Can you feel inner Power?
7. Are you expressing your Power outwardly?
8. How can you improve the use of your Power?

9. If you desire Power for good cause, it will be given.

10. Consider how you could use additional strength.

Relationships

All relationships generate power. It is the magnetism of Power that attracts one person to the other. The bond that holds the relationship is the merging of each other's individual Power. When one partner exerts more than his share, we may see an eruption of some kind. The balance of Power makes the relationship long-standing, in nations and men alike. Using Power with self-control is the ultimate use, producing exciting results. Using Power to control others against their will creates resentment and other deteriorating factors. This vibratory aspect is generally related to material Power. The skillful energy to be both knowledgeable and successful is an exhilarating Power destined to be used with Wisdom. With this Inner Key, you may expect opportunities for success and achievement. These opportunities must be used with care.

Talents

When this vibratory aspect is associated with talent it suggests recognition and reward. An increase of energy in this area can be very promising. Be alert for unexpected opportunities.

If you are presently involved in developing plans, make sure your concentration and efforts are controlled. This type of energy is forceful, and if not used properly, it can be converted to frustration and threaten other channels of expression.

Personal

Receiving a level of Power in this category requires caution. Coming directly into your personal control is a Power to improve and progress. Keep your mind on these types of issues. This is a forceful energy that clears and makes way for positive and successful results. This forceful energy is not negative, but unless it is used correctly, it could appear so. If you apply it to personal relationships where there is an existing weakness, it could demolish the association on a personal basis. Using it for business or material things requires common sense to bring good results.

Business

It is here that the vibratory aspect of 8 can generate positive and successful energy. A sense of power and command in business can be used to improve, change and increase your opportunities.

A feeling of expansion creates the impetus for increase and reward, like heading a large corporation or being promoted to a much-wanted position, with an increase in money and prestige. This vibratory aspect is evident in all areas. In the home, it could mean an increase of money, enabling you to purchase a desired item. Wherever you are in life, this powerful aspect will find you.

EXERCISE 28: INNER KEY 9—RELEASE

RELEASE: To set free from restraint and confinement. To liberate, to set free from obligation, pain, grief, worry. Relief from undesirable situations. To give up, let go.

Self

This beautiful vibration allows a rebirth of new and exciting possibilities. It is important to take advantage of this vital energy. The 9 carries a promise but requires something from you first!

The Key Word is *Release*, and to experience the gift of the 9, you must first Release undesirable conditions on your present life path. This is not always easy, but it is necessary before you can partake in all the 9 offers.

Because the 9 works this way, it is often misunderstood. This energy needs clearance, enough "space" to activate its power in your life. Holding on to unwanted situations, relationships that are no longer working, does not allow room for new and exciting situations, or good and loving relationships. This does *not* mean we should let go of everything that represents security and love. Simply recognize stagnant situations, unnecessary obligations, and anything that you have outlived, which is no longer a part of your future life path.

SEARCHING FOR AN ANSWER:

1. What is missing from your life?
2. Do you know why?
3. Can you recognize the self-made obstacles?
4. To let go requires faith in your own future.
5. The fear that makes you cling can be replaced.
6. Do you know what your fears are?
7. Physical health improves tremendously when you Release negativity.
8. The karmic path becomes clearer with such Release.
9. Release negativity and relationships become even better.
10. A predominance of 9's in dreams or charts means "new life."

Relationships

There may be a tendency to resist the "letting go" aspect of the 9 in the area of relationships. Let me assure you that you are not meant to discard indiscriminately all existing relationships. That would be foolish. The point is that if you are engulfed in relationships that are constantly draining, you should reevaluate them and make adjustments.

This will result in your having more energy, and you can be more discerning in the future. It also allows you to give more time to the relationships that really do matter. And it opens a new vista of possibility for new, meaningful relationships.

Talents

Here is a chance to discard old, tired methods. If you have a strong focus in the area of talent, consider your present efforts and be open to new, more lucrative, ideas. If you have been procrastinating, hiding your talents, the 9 energy will provide the force you need to unveil your talents and improve the way you present yourself. A seed of an idea may suddenly flower into activity with the impact of the 9 energy. Be open and ready for new ideas and expansion of expression.

Personal

The way the 9 energy touches you is personally. You may become discontent with practically everything! You may feel a sense of irritation and self-questioning, asking yourself why this and why that. You may feel a need to start fresh again in many things, reorganize your life, try new things. All these are signs of the 9 energy coming in on a personal level. It can be seen in insignificant situations. Personal appearance may change, with a different style and a new bold approach.

You may find yourself thinking of new work situations, a new residence, new ideas. The only thing that could hold you back would be clinging to present situations.

Business

The message of the 9 is Release. The changes needed are quite evident. You can't make mistakes. Everything you have suppressed rises to the surface when this vibrant energy comes in. Release can be just a matter of changing unwanted situations. The release of the old allows the birth of the new. This is not a disregard for everything you have built or planned. It is a new energy that can help you actually reach these goals, by expanding your plans to fit. Sometimes karma has a way of pushing you to where you are supposed to be in every aspect of your life. If this happens, don't resist, go with the beautiful energy of the 9.

EXERCISE 29: INNER KEY *11—VISION

VISION: The act, power or faculty of sight. The inherent ability to imagine, visualize and prepare for the future. Power of prophecy, especially the vision to look ahead.

Self

The Master *11 Vibration has a unique spiritual power. Under the influence of the Master *11 you can probe within the levels of Consciousness. Much clarity is given through this vibratory force. Often you gain insight, new attitudes, and new and refreshing energy.

When the Master *11 appears in your dream or Gnothology chart it is there for a definite reason! Each time you come to a karmic crossroad in life, the *11 will play a big part in helping you understand your position. Decisions are associated with this vibratory level—serious decisions that can have a long-standing effect. The secret here is to avoid taking the easy way out. It is tempting to bypass future possibilities, to ignore the possible consequences of today's action or lack of action. As the Master *11 seeps through your Consciousness, it will provide a much wider vision of present happenings.

The *11 has a broad scope and brings the capacity for Wisdom. Experiences from past lives are all part of this Higher knowledge. It is difficult to ignore. Each lifetime is a living reminder of previous lifetimes, in that the soul finds itself in similar situations. Sometimes you will find yourself once again surrounded with the same souls, trying to solve or correct or manifest conditions that are an integral part of your ongoing karma.

SEARCHING FOR AN ANSWER:

1. Be sure to consider all things when the *11 is evident.

2. The negative tendency is to become depressed, and/or immobile.

3. Recognize the opportunity to probe, investigate and renew.

4. Examine all aspects of life, especially relationships.

5. Listen to the inner voice of Wisdom and be open.

6. Follow your inner guidance and don't be afraid to try.

7. You need time alone to gather your thoughts.

8. Discover the karmic message you have at this time.

9. Can you recognize your karmic relationships and obligations?

10. Know that, with this energy, you can receive all you need.

Relationships

Through the Master *11 the true nature and purpose of all relationships is revealed. It is unwise to reject what you receive. Perhaps you have not put sufficient energy in some relationship. Heed the urge to correct and make right. Your feeling of love will be amplified where there is cause. You may question particular circumstances. And if so, you will receive the answers. The quality of this Master Vibration opens every facet of your life. The choice to stop and look is entirely within your Wisdom.

Talents

When we look at the area of talent, we usually come face-to-face with hard reality. If you are busily pursuing something that is not complementary, you will be made acutely aware of this.

If you have some doubts about your talent, the Master *11 will give you insight. Consider the *11 as an additional sensitive tool to gain perspective and put your life in order. As you become more alert, you may dream prolifically and be attuned to past-life situations.

Personal

As you enter the Master *11 energy you will immediately feel inner changes. Your sensitivity is increased and you have an extended Vision of what is happening around you. Be open to this, for the negative tendency is to withdraw. This would only add pressure to any existing problems. Be sure to meditate and make the best use of this period. During meditation and sleep you will be more attuned to the Higher Self. This is a good time to truly analyze your own position in life and to be open for new and exciting opportunities.

Business

The Master *11 brings the new broom that sweeps clean. This is a time when you feel ready to express new ideas and put them into action. Any form of study and analysis is excellent now. You may be surprised at what you see, and wonder why you haven't seen it before. If your business requires extended Vision, you will certainly be given this. Small details will be important. What was originally considered insignificant will now become part of your priorities. You will feel a great urge to put everything in order. You will need to see exactly what is going on in every area. On those occasions when the boss decides to do these things, you can be sure he is experiencing the Master *11.

EXERCISE 30: INNER KEY *22—CONTROL

CONTROL: To check, to regulate. The act or power of controlling. To dominate, restrain. To be in command.

Self

This type of Control is not to be confused with oppression or dominance over others. The Master *22 is a Control you gain after mastering and accomplishing certain spiritual requirements. This gift may well spill over into other areas of your life. This, of course, is greatly beneficial. The Master *22 is a surge of power given to you to be used effectively for specific reasons. As this high energy floods your Consciousness, you will feel inspiration and strength.

Unlike the subtle tones of the *11, the Master *22 is vigorous and abundant as it spears your present life activity. There is a sense of urgency surrounding this force. Thought patterns increase and plans for the future are keen to be expedited. Both physical and mental powers are expanded. The body appears to be rejuvenated and the mind demolishes previous obstacles. Every advantage should be taken when you experience the Master *22.

Receiving the Master *22 in a dream denotes that you are entering a period in life where you can enjoy the results of past labor. The success of this vibratory level will be felt on all levels of Consciousness. This means increased good health, a greatly improved mental outlook, and prosperity on a material level.

SEARCHING FOR AN ANSWER:

1. The vibratory sequence is crucial; you need to Control.
2. Consider all aspects of life; this brings the ultimate success.
3. Stay on target, as there is more to come on all levels.
4. Use your increased energy to control all interests.
5. The negative side of *22 is destruction and loss.
6. Become adjusted, and accept the revitalizing power of *22.
7. Check your plans and see that your goals are now in view.
8. Are you ready to use this power well?
9. Can you see beyond your limitations?
10. Feel the inner Control and express it outwardly.

Relationships

Be patient with those around you. Understand that they are not feeling the same rush of energy. Avoid trying to Control others. Direct this energy to yourself. Only by establishing self-control will you enjoy the fruits of the Master level. Think before you act, and conserve and focus your energy. All levels are open to true success. Your personality may tend to be domineering, and this can affect your relationships. Take care and you will receive all the support you need.

Talents

This is a time when your talents become quite evident. You are able to attract those things you need. Try not to be impatient. Put your energy into the vision before you. The urge to be demonstrative must be accompanied with good common sense. Success is all around you; wait until you see it clearly. Be sensitive and alert to all opportunities.

Personal

Avoid extravagance and overspending. Allow the prosperity vibrations to solidify. Your personality will feel exuberant with this vibratory level. Enjoy it by all means, but try not to overshadow others. Your apparent burst of energy will make room for expression. Keep your focus on yourself and your own affairs. Watch the many changes around you, and make wise decisions. Your health will improve but make sure you have sufficient sleep.

Business

Use business acumen. Avoid irrational decision-making. Remember the basic rules of business before you attempt to instigate change. You are poised on the verge of success. You must retain your good business sense. Establish financial security and maintain Control in all aspects of your work. Because this vibratory level reveals the joy of future possibility, you must carefully stay within your original plan until it is cemented. Do not hesitate if you are asked to negotiate or present ideas. Keep your enthusiasm under Control, and let others see your proficiency. You may be asked to take additional responsibility that will take you closer to your goal.

EXERCISE 31: INNER KEY *33—SUCCESS

> SUCCESS: Achievement, obtaining recognition. Improvement of position in life. Satisfactory attainment of goals.

Self

The vibrant Master Number *33 is the solidification of Success. It is reaching a position that is secure and desirable. It is the consummation, the completion of many goals. Spiritually, it is the awakening of the Higher Self. It is the ability to extend your Consciousness into all things—an open and direct channel to every aspect of being. It is the power to be successful.

Existing with awareness is seeing beyond earthly reason, and manifesting this wisdom in all things. We see the Masters operating this way and admire all that they do. This energy force has to be understood and used exactly as it is destined. Misuse of this energy destroys the roots and foundations. The negative aspect breaks down all the possibilities of what might have been. History has shown how great powers on earth have been eliminated through abuse of power. The Master *33 works in the same way.

Inevitably, we can see the diligence and careful planning that is required before the *33 becomes effective. It behooves everyone to have a constant goal, so that when they experience this vibratory force they can see the transformation that takes place in their life. The power of the Master *33 is experienced according to the measure of prior intent, plans and preparation. When there is no evidence of these qualities, the force reduces itself to the energy of the 6, as it cannot exist or prosper unless the foundation is there.

The same is true for the numbers *11 and *22, which would be reduced to the 2 and 4, respectively. Herein we can see the Law of the

Universe at work. The flowering of any endeavor has to be in accordance with the original seed.

SEARCHING FOR AN ANSWER:

1. This intensive level is obtainable if we prepare.
2. Dreams on this level are extremely meaningful.
3. Consider where you are, and analyze accordingly.
4. The *33 has a strong karmic influence and brings change.
5. Are you prepared to enjoy the fullest benefit of *33?
6. Do you have specific goals and plans for the future?
7. Be ready to use the *33. It comes when needed most!
8. It is the culmination of desire and true Success.
9. It is the Master teacher; Success; perfect relationship.

Relationships

Karmic relationships are emphasized under the vibratory influence of *33. In this energy, relationships can prosper. They can also disintegrate, if they are not conducive to your karmic destiny. This powerful energy means Success in all areas. It motivates the original karmic intent, so it produces according to your original plan. It will remove any impediment and replace it, according to your original desire. Possible marriage or divorce are scrutinized, because the soul is looking for the perfect relationship. The Master *33 can accelerate a union and will do so if it finds no resistance. It will also enlarge your vision and make you look objectively at each present relationship. If it is good, it will be improved. If it is negative, the forces will help you to let go.

Talents

This is an excellent time to express hidden talents. A Master Vibration has its strength in karmic roots. A child might show especially remarkable talent when he is under the influence of Master *33.

Personal

The intensity of this high vibratory force is felt on all levels and you can use this energy in all aspects of your life. Its impact is a karmic power, and can be used to express yourself well. Skill and fame come with the Master *33. If you have a vocation to teach, you can become a Master teacher. When the *33 touches your life, you have the power to turn things around, discard the superfluous, and concentrate on manifesting your desires.

Business

You have the opportunity to put things in balance, to make changes so many will gain. You have tremendous leadership qualities and you must use them in the best way possible. This is a time of Success in reaching the peak of your inner desire. The seeds now flower. It may be your karmic purpose to lead others. Much responsibility can arise with the Master *33. You could find the perfect new position, or receive a promotion. The opportunity that comes with the Master *33 can only be used according to the plans you have previously established.

TRANSFORMATION OF NUMERICAL MASTER LEVELS

The Master Numbers of *11, *22 and *33 are similar to electricity, in that they need to be grounded to the earth. These cycles come as a result of the soul's progress, and they are influenced by your capacity to receive. If a soul lacks spiritual balance, the incoming Master energy is transformed—not to a lesser energy, but a different energy, which the soul can use to improve its present status. The Master level is transformed to the energy of its reduced number. Then it is important to reevaluate and resolidify at the level of the reduced number. If the individual handles this opportunity well, then Universal Law automatically pushes him again to the energy level of the Master Number.

The *11 is reduced to 2: FOCUS on cooperation and relationships.

The *22 is reduced to 4: FOCUS on discipline, foundations and principles.

The *33 is reduced to 6: FOCUS on balance and harmony.

The transformation of the Master Number is determined by the Consciousness and its needs at the time. As all numerical vibrations are in constant flux, we become receptive according to our need. If it is vital that we discipline our life and establish firm roots, then the 4 would be more appropriate than the Master Number *22. So the transformation is not based on being worthy or not, but on the soul bringing to itself the vibratory nourishment needed at the time.

There is, however, a crucial point during the transformation period. It is determined by the willingness to allow the transformation. All men have free will on their individual karmic path and they can extend this will to the receptivity of cycle influence. On receiving the impact of a Master cycle one feels the immediate surge of power that accompanies the cycle. If there is a reluctance to adapt, and the recipient elects to retain the energy even though it cannot adapt to the high frequency, a different transformation takes place: the negative aspect becomes prominent, resulting in the negative expression of a Master energy. This, of course, can be instantly stopped at any time. It requires effort to maintain this negative level and it would take an exceptionally negative person to accomplish this. Retaining the negative aspect of a Master Number is not commonplace. You need not be deeply concerned, as it would take extreme negative power to hold this level.

It is quite easy to determine whether or not you are availing yourself of the Master levels. Look back at the Index of the Inner Keys and see the Key Words which define the nature of each energy level. There is sufficient contrast in the Inner Keys to determine whether or not, for example, you are in the influence of the *11 or the 2.

The power and influence of numerical cycles in daily activities and during sleep are precise esoteric instruments that help the seeking mind understand the continuous activity of the Conscious levels. When we are awake, another level sleeps. When we sleep, another level is awake.

CHAPTER NINETEEN

WE NEVER SLEEP

Have you ever considered that a part of you is always awake? The soul has to experience every second of life. The unsleeping Consciousness is always alert, and recording for all time, the activity of the soul as it follows its karmic path. What part of us wakens in the morning and participates in daily life? What part of us yearns for love? Do we wander the universe as idle poets looking down below for the light of a soul mate? Does this happen? Can it happen?

If sleep cuts us away from reality then where do we go in the night? If our Consciousness were to fall asleep at the same time as the physical body then we would experience the transition we know as death. Surely in these six-to-eight hours we are involved in far greater things. Six-to-eight minutes in a waking state becomes a long boring period if we are not properly occupied. We learn to use our time well and consider it wasted if not properly used. So the question is, what fascinating occupation waits for us as we drift away to another level? In the swift return to Consciousness we try to capture memories, retaining symbols and collecting images that refuse to speak or acknowledge the questions of the Conscious mind.

Are we able to inspire one another as we soar into unknown planes? Do we find our love, discover our babies, in our nightly journey to the stars? Do we grasp a substance that slips through our fingers as we slowly awake? Perhaps we unravel the mysteries from the stars, extracting reality from the mystical light patterns. In this light are we exposed to reality? Have we touched the astral Consciousness of new ideas and motivations?

How much do we limit ourselves by focusing everything we are during the hours when we are awake? How much of this requires effort? Does this constant effort reflect on the physical body? This thing we call "age," is it not a foolish term to justify a limited state of existence? Are we not all ageless? Why do we choose a word to explain the constant life force? Why is a flower never thought of as being old? We see the tree through centuries of myth. How did it acquire its royal title of wisdom?

When did your Consciousness last celebrate a birthday? Does physical birth become the one birthday of the soul—and are there not candles much taller and brighter in the heavens? Are these questions to be answered? Who will? Who can? Are they my questions or are they your questions? Might we have collided in the night and fused together that part of us that never meets? Who is to judge the intelligence of un-answered questions?

Is it a heavenly being that weaves a continual mystery through the night? Or is it that other part of self, which seeks for its true existence and purpose? What is this continual mystery that entices the sleeping and awakened Consciousness? Is it you, is it me? Are we the source of the mystery, or the mystery itself?

Perhaps life is intended for us to experience another kind of love, another kind of laughter. Maybe it is a make-believe existence, where we feel lonely and without companions. This thing called "pain" is a reminder that we are really limited—*and* we are more than all these things. Like children playing, we are growing up amid the stars. We are never lonely for we see each other's light. When eyelids finally close and the body mechanism is breathing like a machine, perhaps we escape and create reality because we are free.

Does our individuality merge in the heavens and reluctantly separate to complete the karmic course? Where is the place we dis-covered as children? When we hid beneath the sheets and blankets, from which world were we escaping? Is the comfort of the pillow and the dark warmth of the bed a tiny hole where we escape? We are conceived, born and die in this safe place. It is the gateway to the Universe.

"THE PEAK"

There's a part of a mountain that has to be me,
There's a wave in the ocean, not part of the sea.
A breeze through a doorway, that smile on a face,
Is the way that I am and I cannot replace.

There's a place that I know where I've never been,
There's a star in the sky, that I've never seen.
A prayer from a man, who's lonely and old,
A story I've read but never have told.

There's children I love and words cannot say,
There's things that I feel from my yesterday.
A hope that is worn, with tears and with toil,
A feeling of home, the feel of the soil.

There's a wish I don't know, perhaps it is mine,
There's a dream yet to dream and everything's fine.
A yearning to speak of things in my heart,
The distance of thought, the miles far apart.

There's a prayer that I pray for you and for me
There's a picture of heaven and how things could be.
A need deep inside when I try to speak
It's that part of the mountain, I know it's the peak.

—Eileen Connolly

BRIDGE OF LEARNING

In this series of guidebooks we explore the basic rudiments of esoteric philosophy. Opening doors of old and new possibilities, we explore the vast continent of mystical knowledge. From these precepts, you will have the foundations on which to build your own theories, from your own experience.

Students and teachers alike can use these books as tall firm pillars surrounding their place of learning. Like the ancient scholars, you can enjoy study, practice, and the application of what you learn. These mystical paths, the labyrinthian sources will allow you to explore freely and discover that which you seek.

Through the years and through my written works I have been teacher to so many. As we draw into the fertile place of learning we will see the strong pillars upholding forever the foundations and origin of our need. Between these pillars there are no walls. The sun shines brilliantly through, and allows the breeze to play on our levels of Consciousness. If we listen carefully, we will hear the ocean of spirit—the tide of truth persistent as it touches the sands of time.

Wherever you are, whatever part of the world you live in, we are together in this place, joined by Spirit and purpose. If you feel the urge to study and explore I am always here at this place, within the pillars. Through all these years I have been privileged to have readers throughout the world. Many of you have become proficient and use your knowledge to help others. For reasons unknown I am honored by students who are consistent scholars. Time has increased this student/reader body. Some have progressed to teaching my works and again I feel honored.

In recognizing these things silently I realized it must be shared with you, my reader. To the new reader, I welcome you and hope your search will bring you within the pillars. Let me extend an invitation to you all. If you are interested in being recognized as a Connolly scholar please write to me and I will be pleased to acknowledge this.

Our journey will go on and we will cross many bridges. The humble thoughts of this author become your inheritance. My thoughts are like crumbs I scatter to the winds and with gentle prayer and watchful smile I wait on the Bridge of Learning to see you fly and soar to the highest Peak.

FUTURE GUIDEBOOKS

This series of guidebooks will take us over many bridges. As you approach each new canyon of learning, I will be waiting for you and we will cross yet another bridge. This is the journey of the esoteric scholar.

In each phase of study, you will be more informed. As you cross each bridge you will be more adept. Knowledge brings confidence. It will show in everything you do. The calmness that comes with the light of learning is felt by all. Recognize that wisdom is for those who seek and understand. Learn to use your knowledge well and you will always feel the comforting and satisfying energy that fills the aura when all levels of Consciousness are working together.

For some, wisdom is gained in small pieces and the wise learn how to fit it all together. Knowledge is all connected for it all comes from the same source. The mystery and pleasure of learning is finding how it all works—how it all fits together and how it can never be separated.

APPENDIX: NOTES, TAPES, COURSES

These notes are intended for both teachers and students of meditation. It is important to allow sufficient time for physical and mental relaxation. To reach the required levels you must be in a state of relaxation. Teachers may consider using soft music in the background to facilitate these requirements. Make sure that all clothing is loose and anything that may cause discomfort is removed prior to the relaxation period.

You will see after each statement the word "WAIT." The sensitive teacher will understand what the students are trying to achieve at that particular moment and allow adequate time for them to experience fully each phase of the meditation. The student who undertakes to work alone should also allow sufficient time between each step. When recording the instructions, keep this in mind.

All the meditations in this book are available on tape. They can be used both in classwork and at home.

Dr. Connolly conducts International Certification Courses in the following subjects: Gnothology, Tarot, and esoteric philosophy.

*Lectures
*Workshops
*Intensive Study
*Seminars
*Tapes
*Connolly Tarot Cards

For information on wholesale and retail sales and courses, write to:

Eileen Connolly Associates, Inc.
Route 2, Box 19
Lanexa, VA 23089

If you are unable to find any Newcastle book at your local bookstore, please write to:

Newcastle Publishing Co., Inc.
13419 Saticoy Street
North Hollywood, CA 91605

Please add $2.00 for UPS and handling to the cost of the book for the first book ordered, plus $1.00 for each additional book. California residents please add current sales tax with each order.

Quantity discounts are available to groups, organizations and companies for any Newcastle title. Telephone (213) 873-3191 or FAX your order to Newcastle Publishing Co., Inc. at (818) 780-2007.

Free, complete, current catalogs are available upon request. Just send us your name and address and we will send you a catalog.

Thank you for your interest in Newcastle.

AL SAUNDERS
Publisher